Calligraphic Type Design in the Digital Age

*Let us then go back to the sources of the scribe's art
for new inspirations . . . not indeed to copy those
forms, but to make of them a starting point for new
expressions suited to present day needs.*
Frederic W. Goudy

Just as musicians and artists
seek to create some new expression
of our time and link it to a rich past,
so too must the work of type designers
...remain bound to the great tradition
of the alphabet.

HERMANN ZAPF

Calligraphic Type Design in the Digital Age

An Exhibition in Honor of the Contributions of Hermann and Gudrun Zapf

Selected Type Designs and Calligraphy by Sixteen Designers

Edited by John Prestianni

Presented by the Friends of Calligraphy
San Francisco Public Library
1 September – 31 October 2001

Gingko Press

Calligraphic Type Design in the Digital Age
© 2001 by the Friends of Calligraphy, Inc.
P.O. Box 425194, San Francisco, CA 94142

ISBN 1-58423-096-7
Library of Congress Control Number: 2001092793

First published in the United States of America
in 2001 by Gingko Press Inc.
5768 Paradise Drive, Suite J, Corte Madera, CA 94925

printed and bound in Germany by
Christians Druckerei, Hamburg
and Buchbinderei S.R. Büge, Celle

Contents

Foreword

When we first began dreaming up the idea for this exhibition and catalogue, we were propelled by a few aspirations. One goal was to thank Hermann Zapf and Gudrun Zapf von Hesse for their inspiration to the international community of those who make letterforms, both calligraphic and typographic. However, we wanted to focus specifically on their type designs, rather than presenting an exhibition of their overall efforts in calligraphy, typography, book design, and bookbinding. That had been done before. This time, we wanted to focus on an area of their work that has had a subtle but powerful effect on a vast number of people; for typefaces have an effect not just on those of us who consciously notice their shapes, but on anyone who reads or views them.

Another goal of the exhibition was to give further exposure to the body of type design created by Gudrun Zapf von Hesse. While not as widely known as that of her prolific and celebrated husband, her work is also beautiful and typographically vital, and her career has also been long and productive. And speaking as a woman who has worked for years in a male-dominated type industry, Gudrun Zapf von Hesse's example has given me much inspiration and faith that good work is worth doing.

This exhibition was also a unique opportunity for us to see the work of these two masters together. They approach design problems differently and independently, their type designs have been developed by different foundries, and they even work on two different floors of their home in Darmstadt, Germany. Yet their marriage has surely had a symbiotic effect on their work, and the respect and affection of one for the work of the other is felicitously apparent. Here is another inspirational model. I wonder whether it has been love and proximity that has kept their individual artistic pursuits vibrant, or whether their mutual preoccupation with letterforms has helped to keep their marriage strong over so many years. Probably both.

The final goal of this exhibition was to show the impact of calligraphic forms on contemporary type design. The work of Hermann Zapf and Gudrun Zapf von Hesse has helped to light the way for many type designers who have used calligraphy as a basis for their designs. Two prominent trends are noticeable in type design sales over the last twenty-five years. One is the continuing success of cool, constructed faces like Helvetica and Futura, and the other is the continuing success of calligraphic faces like Optima and Palatino. And as I write this in the year 2001, script typefaces are also selling briskly. This may mean that despite the dominance of machines and technology in our lives, and the satisfaction that machines can bring, we still respond to forms that clearly come from the human hand. We respond to forms that carry a reminder of our living, breathing bodies and our passionate souls. It's curious – yet wonderful – that we still use the word "hands" to describe calligraphy styles, and the word "faces" to describe type styles. There is something magical about making letters with our own hands, there is something magical about watching someone write with pleasure and brio, and there is something magical about type designers who base their work on calligraphy.

In the process of making this book and mounting the exhibition, many people lent their hands to help. On behalf of the Friends of Calligraphy, I would like to thank those who gave their time, expertise, love, support, and magic: Patricia Akre, Brian Allen, Kim Bach, Harold Berliner, Sam Berlow, John D. Berry, Suellen Bilow, Alan Blackman, Erik van Blokland, Fred Brady, Larry Brady, Janice Braun, Debbie Brawner, Jane Brenner, Robert Bringhurst, Kathleen Burch, John Burns, Mo Cohen, Christine Colasurdo, John Crichton, Rick Cusick, Georgia Deaver, Judy Detrick, Claude Dieterich, Gary van Dis, Timothy Donaldson, Paul Hayden Duensing, Ward Dunham, Everett Erlandson, Jean Evans, Dan Forster, Tony Forster, Marcia Friedman, Helen Fung, Chuck Geschke, Pete Giarratano, Karyn Gilman, E. M. Ginger, Carter Goodwin, Georgianna Greenwood, Andrea Grimes, Phill Grimshaw, Penny Grimshaw Ogden, Keala Hagmann, Craig Hansen, Jon Harl, John Hawk, Susan Hildreth, Otmar Hoefer, Cynthia Hollandsworth, Steve Jobs, Jerry Kelly, Young Kim, Akira Kobayashi, Peter Koch, Donna Lee, Richard Lipton, Peter Lofting, David Lopes, Sherrie Lovler, Linda Mitchell, John Neal, Katie O'Neill, David Pankow, Harry Parker, Asa Peavy, John Prestianni, Patrick Reagh, Julie von der Ropp, Jackie Sakwa, Marcia Schneider, David Schwabe, Susan Skarsgard, Robert Slimbach, Paul Smith, Viktor Solt-Bittner, Jack Stauffacher, Sumner Stone, Laurie Szujewska, Paul Tatum, Susie Taylor, Melissa Titone, Debby Turrietta, Jovica Veljović, Kathy Walkup, Julian Waters, David Winkler, Nicholas Yeager, Gudrun Zapf von Hesse, and Hermann Zapf.

Linnea Lundquist

Editor's Note

This catalogue is one component of the 2001 Zapfest exhibition sponsored by the Friends of Calligraphy to honor Hermann and Gudrun Zapf for their work in calligraphic type design. Each item loaned by the Zapfs and the fourteen other participating designers is listed, and representative examples are reproduced. These include typeface specimens, applications of the types, developmental work (such as working drawings), and calligraphy. The catalogue is also intended to briefly profile each designer. This has been done through biographical notes, personal statements, and catalogue entries that include many details and circumstances surrounding development and production of the typefaces. When an exhibition item has been illustrated, its catalogue entry number is printed next to the image, and an arrow symbol appears with the text entry.

A number of essays relating to the exhibition and its theme are also presented. The essay illustrations include supplemental pieces that accompanied the exhibition materials, as well as other examples. Thus "Honoring Friends," by Susie Taylor, features original Zapf calligraphy and materials belonging to the Book Arts and Special Collections Center of the San Francisco Public Library. Likewise, in "Calligraphy and Type Design," by Jerry Kelly, we reproduce historic and modern items from the Library's collections. In "Cultivating an Education in Letters," Rick Cusick presents all the calligraphic types designed by the Zapfs for Hallmark Cards. In each of the Zapfs' essays, supplementary items from the exhibition appear. And, in Hermann Zapf's essay, there are representative showings of the typefaces Palatino, Michelangelo, and Sistina, as well as other calligraphic designs not highlighted in the exhibition.

The catalogue entries were written by Susie Taylor, Linnea Lundquist, and myself. I also wrote the biographical notes preceding the exhibition entries for Hermann Zapf and Gudrun Zapf von Hesse. The biographical notes on the other fourteen designers were written by Linnea Lundquist. The bibliography was prepared by Susie Taylor and Andrea Grimes.

It was a privilege to be invited to join the team of talented individuals who committed so much energy, care, and time to the making of this catalogue. I would like to add my personal thanks to those persons who aided me with the task of editing it.

First, to Hermann Zapf and Gudrun Zapf von Hesse, whose generosity in loaning their work, and whose consummate professionalism in presenting it,

both enabled the exhibition and set the standard to be reached for in publishing a catalogue. The essays contributed by the Zapfs are uniquely informative of their working methods and attitudes about calligraphic type design. I am also grateful for the Zapfs' kind cooperation in loaning a number of special items just for this publication.

Next, to Linnea Lundquist and Susie Taylor, who represent the Friends of Calligraphy and the San Francisco Public Library. Their vision and enthusiasm for the exhibition gave shape to much of the catalogue. They spent numberless hours organizing, arranging, and cataloguing the materials, and responded to my frequent, if not daily questions with speed, precision, and thoroughness. I consider them both my co-editors.

To all the essay contributors, but particularly to Rick Cusick, who has explicated the work done by Hermann and Gudrun Zapf for Hallmark Cards, and the significance of that work to the topic of calligraphic type design. Rick is responsible for the rare display of the Zapfs' Hallmark typefaces, and for setting them as a double page specimen. He arranged for permission to reproduce them as well as the Hallmark photos of Hermann Zapf. He also generously gave of his talent and time to produce cover art and a frontispiece, with quotations and types by the Zapfs. To Jerry Kelly, for his historical perspective on calligraphic type design, and for his subsequent aid in obtaining certain illustrations. To Sumner Stone, for his thoughtful reflections on a calligrapher's journey to the field of type design. To Susie Taylor, for her insightful memoir on Hermann Zapf's 1977 exhibition at the San Francisco Public Library; and for her account, as a calligrapher, on learning from and studying with Professor Zapf.

The designers of the catalogue, Jack Stauffacher and Laurie Szujewska, most ably worked with me as all the individual texts were drafted, edited, and paired with their respective illustrations. They are to be thanked for their patience and cooperation, and their commitment to producing an outstanding catalogue design. The exhibition organizers and I are especially grateful to Jack Stauffacher for his assent to help us with the project. To Jovica Veljović, for his generous contribution of photographs of Hermann and Gudrun Zapf. And to our publisher, Mo Cohen of Gingko Press, for his enthusiastic belief in the viability of this catalogue.

John Prestianni

Introduction and Essays

Theo Varlet

AN EDUCATION THROUGH BOOKS

is a companion which no misfortune
can depress — no crime destroy —
no enemy alienate, — no despotism
enslave.

* At home, a friend; abroad an
introduction; in solitude, a solace;
and in society an ornament.

Without books, what is man ?

script: Hermann Zapf

Susie Taylor   Introduction:
                       Honoring Friends

As much as anything else, the exhibition "Calligraphic Type Design in the Digital Age," is about relationships: relationships between people, and relationships that people have with letters and their forms. It is about a husband and a wife, Hermann Zapf and Gudrun Zapf von Hesse, and their work as type designers and calligraphers. It is about a generation of type designers working today who acknowledge the example and influence of the Zapfs, and for whom calligraphy is a meaningful inspiration in the design of new types. In a larger sense, it is about the great number of people interested in calligraphic type design: they are calligraphers, graphic designers, artists, typophiles, biblio-philes, and others who care about the aesthetics of the written or printed word. And it is about friendships: the friendships of colleagues, of students and teachers, patrons and artists. Perhaps it is these friendships that are most telling in the exhibition.

I am a calligrapher as well as curator of a calligraphy collection in a public library. My first real introduction to the Zapfs began in 1977. I had just started working in the Special Collections Department of the San Francisco Public Library. In November 1977, the Library, with the Friends of Calligraphy (FOC), hosted Hallmark Cards' traveling exhibition of Hermann Zapf's work. Anne Englund, the librarian who then headed Special Collections, arranged this. It was a heady experience when we opened the packing boxes to discover the rich variety of calligraphic and typo-graphic works. The show was large and filled the library's exhibition spaces on two floors. One of the exhibition events included a panel discussion about Professor Zapf's work by Jack Stauffacher, Adrian Wilson, Theo Jung, Andrew Hoyem and Sumner Stone. These men – all respected professionals in fine printing, book design, calligraphy or type design – gathered to talk about the man whose work was dis-played. This, to me, underscored the regard in which Hermann Zapf was held by his peers.

But long before the 1977 exhibition at the Library, I knew something about Hermann Zapf's work. I had begun to do calligraphy in 1969. Then, I took private lessons from Byron J. Macdonald, the San Francisco

Gudrun Zapf von Hesse and Hermann Zapf.
Photo by Jovica Veljović, June 2001.

lettering artist. The lessons were held in his offices on Kearny Street, where he maintained a lettering studio. One day, I noticed a poster hanging on the studio wall. It was Hermann Zapf's 1959 pen drawn alphabet of large roman majuscules in asymmetrically arranged lines, surrounded by quotations written in roman minuscule, italic, blackletter, and Greek. I distinctly remember a sense of electric connection, of discovery at seeing such beautiful writing, so perfectly executed, in a strong, elegant design. It seemed to belong to an-other, and higher, order of accomplishment.

In those years it was not so easy to find one's way to the best sources of study. I was fortunate to be able to take lessons with Byron Macdonald, who was a gifted and accomplished scribe. As well as teaching me tech-nical matters, he pointed me in a certain direction, and I began to find my way to those sources that most in-spired me. Over time, I found that it was the work of Hermann Zapf that most drew my eye. I kept coming back to examples of his calligraphy, with its beautiful, if challenging forms, so sophisticated in their propor-tions and details, displaying their lineage of the best of the classic scripts. Like many others before and since, I became enamored of the work of Hermann Zapf. To me, it set a kind of standard to which I should aspire.

Working with the calligraphy and printing history materials in Special Collections, I had many more re-sources for study. Again, the work of Hermann Zapf exerted its attraction on me. Besides his printed publi-cations, the Library owns two rare examples of origi-nal Zapf calligraphy: "An Education Through Books," commissioned by William Holman, and an informal

Facing page, left. Hermann Zapf. "An Education Through Books." Original calligraphic broadside. Ink and watercolor on paper. Commissioned by William Holman for the Harrison Calligraphy Collection, San Francisco Public Library. 1966. 20 x 14 inches.

Two engraved metal printing plates for *Pen and Graver*. Roman Capitals and Humanistic Cursive. Calligraphy by Hermann Zapf, cut in metal by August Rosenberger, punchcutter at D. Stempel AG typefoundry. San Francisco Public Library. 5.75 x 10.25.

alphabet presented by Professor Zapf to the late Theo Jung, the book designer. Jung was the source for many of the Zapf items in the Library collections – books, type specimens, prints, even handwritten correspondence. In showing these to library patrons, I had the opportunity to study them and, not infrequently, to learn more through discussions with persons more knowledgeable than myself. As I began to learn more about typography, I took notice of the work of Gudrun Zapf von Hesse, who was not then as well known as her husband, but whose typefaces were often to be found in his books and typographic specimens. The pages of Diotima from Liber Librorum, seen in this exhibition, were a happy discovery. I also remember finding a small catalogue illustrated with examples of her bookbinding, from a rare joint exhibition with her husband, held in Stockholm in 1952.

The 1970s and 1980s also saw a popular rise of interest in calligraphy. Calligraphy societies formed in major cities across the United States. Teachers of prominence – American, English, and European – traveled from city to city offering seminars and classes. Communication between the local societies increased rapidly as a result, and it wasn't long before national calligraphy conferences became an annual event in different locations each year. Many new books on the subject were published, and calligraphic instruction even found its way to the television screen.

The impetus to seek instruction directly from Professor Zapf was strong. He had taught calligraphy at one time in Germany, at the Werkkunstschule Offenbach. And he had instructed lettering artists at Hallmark Cards in Kansas City, Missouri. Although he was not involved in the popular activities sponsored by the American calligraphy societies, it was possible to apply to attend the summer courses he taught at the Rochester Institute of Technology (RIT). I first heard about the program in 1978, from Terry McGrath, who had attended the very first session. However, I had to wait until 1982, when I traveled to Rochester with my friend and fellow calligrapher John Prestianni, to attend Professor Zapf's calligraphy course.

Whatever trepidation we had about studying with Professor Zapf was quickly dispelled by his friendly and courteous demeanor and his obvious respect and love for his subject. Always there was an atmosphere of collegiality in the classroom, as Professor Zapf lectured, demonstrated and answered the many questions from students. We studied formal roman majuscules and other hands. Professor Zapf would go from student to student offering individual instruction and demonstration. He shared his working methods freely. Some of these "tips and tricks" (as he called them) are recorded in my class notes and include the following: use a small, stiff haired artist's brush to barely fill the nib of the pen with hand ground sumi stick ink, because the stiff bristles will clean the nib of drying ink while filling it with fresh ink; don't use paper that is too smooth, the pen needs a little resistance from the paper to produce sharp strokes; write with varied pressure to create tapered strokes; hold the pen up at a very steep angle for better control, especially when writing small letters; when retouching calligraphy with white gouache, match the white pigment exactly to the color of the paper so it can't be seen; in making serifs on roman letters, use only one prong of the nib, working quickly, or use a smaller nib size.

Of equal if not greater significance was Professor Zapf's fundamental attitude about writing and working. This became apparent as the course progressed. It was often summed up in brief but telling statements. His seemingly simple proposition, "Do it all nicely from the beginning – everything" made me realize the importance of taking seriously all the various steps involved in producing calligraphy. I remember his caution about the study of historic letterforms, and the importance of using such models mainly for inspiration. One should not copy them precisely, because the world and time in which they were created are so different from our own. A slavish imitation of historic forms cannot answer today's needs.

In 1983, John and I returned to take the typography course. This was a comprehensive treatment of historic forms, contemporary methods, and issues on the subject of the design and use of type. The class was small, and all of us spent much time together, talking about calligraphy and type, and the examples Professor Zapf spoke of in his lectures. We were frequently to be found in the Cary Library, where librarian David Pankow and Professor Zapf presented many treasures. And there was time for recreational activity. I will never forget a class outing we took one weekend, when the rodeo came to Rochester.

Many friendships resulted from the courses at Rochester. There remains a bond of shared experience with others who attended: from the San Francisco Bay Area, including Georgia Deaver, Claude Dieterich, Linnea Lundquist, and Terry McGrath; and with calligraphers from all over the country, among them Julian Waters, Jerry Kelly, Marcy Robinson, and John Stevens.

In the following years, we again met Professor Zapf, and were introduced to Gudrun Zapf von Hesse, when the couple visited San Francisco. The Zapfs numbered several friends here, including Jack Stauffacher and the late Adrian Wilson. The most memorable encounter was a Sunday in 1983. We spent an afternoon in Special Collections with the Zapfs and their hosts Adrian and Joyce Wilson, examining highlights of the collection. It was a privilege to be included in their

Hermann Zapf and August Rosenberger. Hand colored title page of *Das Blumen-ABC* (The Flower Alphabet). Brush drawings of flowers by Hermann Zapf, made 1943–1946 and cut in lead by August Rosenberger, punchcutter at D. Stempel AG typefoundry. San Francisco Public Library. 13 x 9.5 inches.

conversation about the past and present of typography and book design. I recall that Professor Zapf raised an issue relating to modern type design by comparing the grid system used at that time to an illustration in Albrecht Dürer's treatise on lettering, of 1525. Following that visit, and continuing to this time, the Zapfs have gifted the Library with generous donations of books, prints and other examples of their work, many of which would otherwise be unobtainable.

In 1984, Professor Zapf was made an Honorary Member of the Friends of Calligraphy. The Honorary Membership was awarded as an expression of respect and esteem for his accomplishments over a lifetime dedicated to beautiful letters. The text of the Friends' letter to him on this occasion reads, in part: "The excellence of your calligraphy serves to inspire, and awakens in our own minds and hearts a greater understanding, appreciation and love of letters."

This exhibition was conceived to honor both Hermann Zapf and Gudrun Zapf von Hesse. To mark the event, the Friends of Calligraphy has conferred a Lifetime Achievement Award to both of the Zapfs, for the inspiration and example they have given to others throughout their careers.

The first proposal for "Calligraphic Type Design in the Digital Age" was made in September 1999. Linnea Lundquist – type designer, calligrapher, and former student of Professor Zapf at RIT – suggested a joint exhibition by Professor Zapf and Gudrun Zapf von Hesse, to demonstrate the connection between calligraphy and type design, to be held at the San Francisco Public Library. Other type designers would also be invited to participate, to show how this connection has motivated others, especially in the last decade. A lecture series was planned, concurrent with the exhibition.

Yes, God JOHN 3:16
loved the world
so much that he
GAVE HIS
ONLY CHILD,
SO THAT ALL
PEOPLE WITH FAITH IN HIM CAN
ESCAPE DESTRUCTION,
AND LIVE FOREVER·

Hermann Zapf. Quotation from Gospel of St. John, chapter 3, verse 16. Original calligraphic broadside of Bible verse, written for 3:16, *Bible Texts Illuminated,* by Donald E. Knuth. Madison, Wisconsin, A-R Editions, 1991. Ink and watercolor on paper. San Francisco Public Library. 12 x 9 inches.

Gudrun Zapf von Hesse. Quotation from 2 Thessalonians,
chapter 3, verse 16. Original calligraphic broadside for *3:16,
Bible Texts Illuminated,* by Donald E. Knuth. Madison, Wisconsin,
A-R Editions, 1991. Watercolor on paper collage. San Francisco
Public Library. 8.5 x 8.5 inches.

The Friends sent an invitation to the Zapfs in the spring of 2000. The Zapfs responded by accepting our proposal, saying, in part, that the suggestion of coming to San Francisco for a joint exhibition was "so unusual that we can't say no." It must be noted what a pleasure it has been to work with the Zapfs to produce the exhibition and to enjoy their support, encouragement, and enthusiasm for our plans.

An invitation to participate was issued to the fourteen other type designers in the exhibition, each of whom accepted the invitation to share their work in honor of the Zapfs. Each designer was asked to provide a specimen of a selected typeface, any background and developmental material, examples of an application of the type, and one of their calligraphic works.

Linnea Lundquist volunteered to chair the Zapfest, as the project was dubbed. Linnea also assumed the task of curating the exhibition, with the help of Sumner Stone and myself. Many others from the Friends and other San Francisco Bay Area book arts groups joined to work on organizing committees. This catalogue was planned, to show selected works from the exhibition and to present articles by the Zapfs and others on calligraphy and calligraphic type design. The eminent book designer and fine printer Jack Stauffacher, who is also Professor Zapf's longtime friend and colleague, was invited to design the catalogue, with his fellow designer Laurie Szujewska. John Prestianni, a past editor of *Alphabet, The Journal of the Friends of Calligraphy,* volunteered his efforts to plan, edit and oversee the catalogue production.

Some words about the Friends of Calligraphy, the sponsor of this exhibition, are in order. The FOC is a non-profit organization founded in 1974 as a result of the renewed interest in calligraphy that took place in this country in the 1970s.

According to its bylaws, the purpose of the Friends is "to promote the study and practice of calligraphy, to encourage individual excellence, to foster a wider appreciation and deeper understanding of calligraphy, its history and applications." Activities have evolved over twenty-five years to include seminars and workshops,

Hermann Zapf. Calligraphic broadside. Italic minuscule alphabet, with majuscule ampersand and initials T, J and Z, written as a keepsake for Theo Jung. Ink and watercolor on Japanese paper. San Francisco Public Library. 1968. 15.25 x 9.75 inches.

lectures, publications, and exhibitions. A dedicated corps of volunteers sustains these efforts.

A long standing association between the FOC and the San Francisco Public Library led to its choice as the exhibition venue. The Library's Marjorie G. and Carl W. Stern Book Arts and Special Collections Center is the location of two collections that are important resources for calligraphers and for the book arts community.

The Harrison Collection of Calligraphy and Lettering, begun as the private collection of San Francisco calligrapher Richard Harrison in the 1950s, features an international selection of contemporary calligraphy, manuscripts and printed works, including a collection of reference material. The accessibility of the collection in a public library prompts use by scribes, teachers and students. It is a destination for calligraphers from around the world.

The collection of San Francisco printer Robert Grabhorn forms the basis for the Grabhorn Collection on the History of Printing and Development of the Book. It contains early printed books, historic printers' manuals, a range of fine press books, printed ephemera and type specimens. The breadth of its reference collection attracts students of printing, papermaking and bookbinding.

It is therefore most appropriate that "Calligraphic Type Design in the Digital Age" is held in the San Francisco Public Library. The exhibition confirms the place that beautiful letters have in written communications. And while it celebrates the successes of the recent past, it also illuminates the direction that letterforms will take in future years. In its creation, the exhibition has brought together many friends and colleagues to honor Hermann Zapf and Gudrun Zapf von Hesse, two individuals whose contributions have enriched the calligraphic and typographic traditions of our time. So many relationships – between teacher and student, typographer and typophile – are thereby affirmed and deepened. We are appreciative, and very grateful.

How do we learn to write? It seems as though it should be simple. We must first start with a good model. We move the pen, trying to imitate the forms. Then we examine the result. Usually the first efforts look pretty bad. Maybe the A leans a bit to the right, or perhaps the crossbar is too low, or the bottom bowl of the B is too big. So we make them again. Sometimes they get better, sometimes worse. Maybe the B is too wide this time, or perhaps the pen angle is wrong.

In fact, writing is not simple. The serious writer must embark on a long course of study and practice. And then, perhaps after many years, an A and a B may appear that seem good. As Edward Johnston, the father of modern calligraphy in England, said, "I have not yet done my best work, and I probably never will."

One learns that one cannot make a perfect copy of the model – any model. In fact, no writer can even make precisely the same letter twice. There are always small variations, little quirks. These frailties in the letters are one aspect of what makes them human. But what makes them good?

Lloyd Reynolds, my first teacher of calligraphy, passed on wisdom from the Chinese tradition. What makes the writing good is not merely making letters which have all the parts in the right place, or the proper proportions, or balance. All of these things are necessary, but they are not sufficient. Spirit, the breath of life, must flow from the writer into the writing. Only then can the writing have the qualities that we admire, not only in letters but also in people. Strength. Beauty. Grace. Poise.

In some cultures – Chinese, Japanese, Arabic – calligraphy is prized for its spiritual quality. Great calligraphers are considered to be great artists just as we in the West give special status to great painters and sculptors.

The study of writing tradition is important, but certain things are learned only through accumulated acts of writing. Letter after letter is made. Each new stroke embodies decisions, feelings. There are triumphs, disappointments, elation, drudgery. By the practice of writing (or any process that involves making letters by hand, such as drawing, cutting or engraving) we gradually acquire a personal tradition of letter making. From the very first stroke we begin a trail of letters. These may in the beginning seem only like unwanted baggage. But in time, as we continue, they become our personal treasury.

The forms we make are expressive not only of our skill in manipulating the tools, but also of our personality, our inner energy, our accumulated experience. This is inescapable.

People frequently want to know how new styles of typefaces emerge. The raw material of a new style can be found in the personal lettering tradition of the writer.

Eric Gill, Edward Johnston's student, stone cutter, sculptor, and type designer, said that letters are things, not pictures of things. Written letters are very spare drawings. A few strokes. It is perhaps this fact that makes the signature of the writer inseparable from the writing itself. Perhaps drawings of landscapes or the human figure are easier to forge. They are much more complex. In the written form there is nowhere to hide.

There is also an impersonal side to letterforms. They are utilitarian objects, intended to be read. We expect them to be familiar, not to depart too radically from the letters we are used to reading every day. The writer is therefore constrained by history. There may be a new A, but it must be very similar to the old As. Letterform invention generally proceeds in small increments.

The mechanization of writing which occurred in the fifteenth century was motivated by utility. Printing multiple copies of a book is cheaper than writing each one by hand. The process of making metal type brought with it new challenges for the letter maker. Each letter, once made, is duplicated in exactly the same form. The spacing of the characters is fixed.

Unlike the calligrapher, the type designer cannot make, or attempt to make, small corrections every time the letter is written. Commitment to the final form of the letter must be taken very seriously. Letter copies have been mechanically accurate since the invention of movable type, and we have now entered an age of even more precise digital duplication. The final form of a character will be relentlessly repeated.

In the first days of metal type, typographic forms were based on the handwriting of the day; there were no other models. Soon, however, they departed from strict copies of manuscript letters and developed their own distinctive structure and aesthetic in the new environment of punchcutting, typecasting, composition and printing.

In the twentieth century we have seen a revival of the craft of calligraphy with the edged pen. This has led, once again, to the design of typefaces based directly on calligraphic forms.

Of course, in order to design calligraphic typefaces, one must first do calligraphy. This is no small matter. Acquiring a good hand is a task that requires, at a minimum, years of devotion. There are benefits, however. The personal tradition that is created by years of letter making, calligraphic or otherwise, is fertile ground for generating genuinely new styles. In this realm the personal, aesthetic aspect is ascendant. A worthwhile new design is not produced by a simple twist, or by some clever trick applied uniformly to an existing alphabet style. A truly new design has a magic that makes it greater than the sum of its parts. Its organic quality springs from the designer's active life of letter making.

The creation of new letterforms requires all the powers of the designer to be focused on the task. Alphabets are systems, and today's typography requires systems of alphabets. The intellect is engaged. Intuition plays an important role. The visual materials from one's accumulated experience in making letters are always in the background. It is a creative act which requires stamina and dedication. One can work very hard and still fail to make a new style that has merit.

The process of turning writing into type means transforming the personal into the impersonal. It means converting a handmade object into one that is ultimately produced by a machine. Frequently it also means making a relatively private work into a much more public one. The calligrapher has complete control over what he or she will write, how it will be composed, and what materials will be used. The type designer passes his or her hard won forms out into the world for anyone to use or abuse.

Producing a good typeface from calligraphic drawings or models is not an automatic process. Usually the machine-made letter has to be re-produced through several generations before it can reappear before the eyes of the reader as type. In most of the period of making metal type, for example, a steel punch was first engraved by hand, a process that requires great skill. The steel punch was then struck into brass to produce a matrix which served as a mold for casting the lead type. The resulting metal letter surface was then covered with ink and pressed onto paper.

Preparation of the masters used by phototypesetting machines involved cutting letterforms by hand from a plastic sheet, another skilled operation, and the modification of letterforms to compensate for optical problems created by the photographic technology of the day.

Creating software that represents the digital type currently in use also requires intricate work. The points that define curves making up the outline shape of the letter must be carefully placed and manipulated, again an operation requiring skill. In order to make the type acceptable for printing at low resolutions, special "hints" must be added to the software.

At every step, one tries to retain as much of the life breath as possible – to capture the spirit and the personality of the written letter – but there is always something about a first generation letter that is more immediate, more direct, more human than any of the generations that follow. A successful new calligraphic typeface, therefore, is a masterful illusion. We believe we are looking at handwriting, but we are looking at typography. Somehow the qualities of the hand, the eye, and the spirit have been preserved through the intricate and potentially brutal process of turning writing into type.

The new typeface is not just a thing, or a collection of things. It is a Form, and each letter is a Form, arrived at through a process of devotion, inspiration and distillation. The letter bodies may be made of metal, of light, of carbon dust, compounds of silver, of paint, vinyl, or even of granite. No matter. In every case we can easily identify them. They are Diotima, or Optima. They have a name. They have a soul. They live in the ether of the human heart and mind. A Type is born.

Jerry Kelly   Calligraphy and Type Design
The Twentieth Century Quest for a Renewed Connection

In his 1923 book *A Brief Survey of Printing History and Practice* (written with Holbrook Jackson) Stanley Morison begins the chapter on printing types with the following: "Handwriting is of course the forerunner of printing." Morison assumed the reader's familiarity with the types of Gutenberg, Schoefer, Jenson, and other fifteenth century printers who modeled their typefaces on the manuscripts of their time. More importantly, at the end of the chapter he asks "who will lead us back to the great sixteenth-century masters [of calligraphy]; Palatino of Rome, Tagliente of Venice, Yçiar of Saragosa, and Beauchesne of Paris? Only then shall we be able to evolve letters and types [that are] original as well as beautiful." There can be little doubt that Morison's plea was answered about a quarter of a century later, in the calligraphy and type designs of Hermann Zapf and Gudrun Zapf von Hesse. Both of the Zapfs are master calligraphers, and their calligraphy has informed their type designs. Yet they have been able to meld their calligraphy into a typographic form – an achievement that other skilled calligraphers have not always attained.

Morison was well aware of the work of several notable type designers of his time. He mentions the types of Ehmcke, Tiemann, and Koch in the same paragraph, quoted above. A few pages further on we find illustrations of two typefaces by the prolific American type designer Frederic Goudy; his typeface Goudy Modern is labeled a "recent successful face" by Morison. Still, we can surmise that the work of these accomplished type designers falls short of displaying the kind of synergy between living calligraphy and practical, original type design which we find in the types of Hermann Zapf and Gudrun Zapf von Hesse and the other designers whose work appears in this exhibition. The types of Ehmcke, Tiemann, Koch and Goudy retain too many of the personal quirks found in handmade letterforms to be generally useful.

The somewhat personal designs of Tiemann, Koch, Goudy, Dwiggins, and others – while often beautiful – rarely proved as acceptable to the printer as the type revivals produced early in the twentieth century. These revivals were based on typeface models by the fifteenth century Jenson and Griffo, the sixteenth century Garamond and Granjon, and the eighteenth century Baskerville and Bodoni. The historic type models were most often based on the living calligraphy of their time, and then adapted for modern manufacture and use. Re-cuttings based on classic fonts

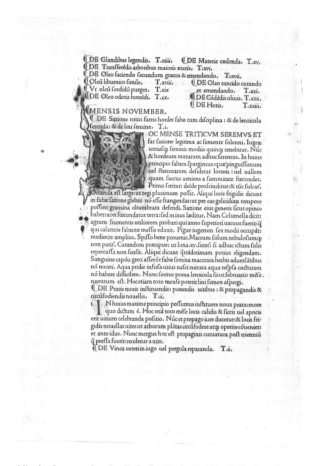

Nicolas Jenson, d. 1480. *De Re Rustica* by Rutilius Palladius, first edition, 1472. Roman type first used in Jenson's *Eusebius* of 1470. Single leaf, printed text with vermilion and ultramarine pen drawn letters and large gilded initial with white vine decoration. San Francisco Public Library. 12.75 x 9 inches.

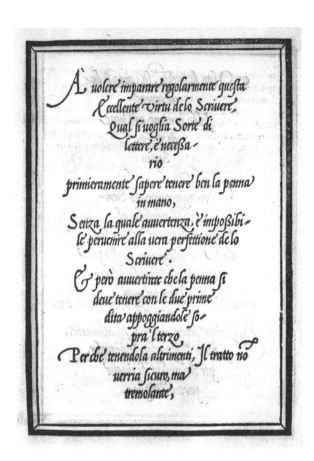

Giovanbattista Palatino. *Libro nuovo d'imparare a scrivere,* 1545 edition. Lettere cancellaresche. Calligraphy reproduced by cutting on wood blocks for printing. San Francisco Public Library. 7.25 x 5 inches.

such as Garamond, Baskerville, Jenson, and the faces made by Francesco Griffo for Aldus Manutius (Morison's personal favorites) were more useful, even for modern purposes, than the often somewhat idiosyncratic contemporary designs of the first half of the twentieth century. The classic forms of the earlier types were adapted to modern type casting technologies, proving quite valuable to printers. This left many fine typographers yearning for contemporary types which could demonstrate some all-around adaptability, particularly for fine book work where more readable types are preferred over novel advertising fonts. Such a desire led Morison, in his capacity as typographic advisor to the British Monotype Corporation, to foster the development and production of contemporary typefaces in addition to his successful series of typeface revivals. Among the modern faces produced as part of his program were Eric Gill's Perpetua, Joseph Blumenthal's Emerson, and Jan van Krimpen's Lutetia design.

Daniel Berkeley Updike also felt that merely reviving earlier styles of type design and typography was inadequate for modern work. In his monumental *Printing Types* he stated that "types have always reflected the taste and feeling of their time." Striving for a contemporary style in typeface design, Updike commissioned two original fonts for exclusive use at his Merrymount Press: Merrymount, designed in 1894 by Bertram Grosvenor Goodhue; and Montallegro, designed in 1904 by Herbert Horne. Neither type can be considered successful, and both were only occasionally used by Updike.

The Golden Type

ABCDEFGHIJKLMNOPQRSTUVWXYZ

1 2 3 4 5 Æ Œ 6 7 8 9 0

a b c d e f g h i j k l m n o p q r s t u v w x y z

æ œ & ff fi fl ffi ffl ! ? (' . , ; : – ‚

William Morris. Specimen of the Golden Type. 1890. San Francisco Public Library. 5.25 x 2.5 inches.

Jan van Krimpen (1892-1958) came closest to answering Morison's call for a return to the master calligrapher informing the type designer. Van Krimpen's first type design, Lutetia, was issued in 1925, two years after Morison's *Survey* was published. Therefore, Lutetia was not under consideration at the time. But twenty-eight years later Morison wrote the foreword to the record of Van Krimpen's work, published in honor of the Dutch designer's sixtieth birthday. There he acknowledged Van Krimpen's mastery and integration of both arts, using the phrase "calligraphy and typography" no less than eight times in the course of a five paragraph essay. Van Krimpen executed all the myriad aspects of the letter arts – calligraphy, type design, typography, and book design – with style and grace.

There are parallels between Van Krimpen and Hermann Zapf. Like Zapf, Van Krimpen worked for a major type foundry where most of his types were manufactured, and where many of his finely printed book designs were produced. Also like Zapf he eschewed the practice of copying old, classic types, and, even worse, imitating old styles of typography. Instead, he professed a modern, contemporary aesthetic. However he was neither avant-garde nor a rebel. On the contrary, Van Krimpen used modern materials and demonstrated an aesthetic that was traditional and classically based. Zapf's work is often more experimental and warm than Van Krimpen's, but both men strove for modern expression within the tradition of classical typography. In this way Van Krimpen's work has much affinity with Zapf's design principles: an open, modern aesthetic, not harking back to an earlier time; manifesting itself mainly in three key areas of the graphic arts: calligraphy, type design, and book design. Zapf too would bring new expression to these areas.

Zapf's first type, a fraktur christened Gilgengart, had a long and torturous birth. Accepted by the Stempel foundry in 1939, the release of Gilgengart was delayed by the War and Hitler's irrational edict against blackletter types. When Gilgengart was finally ready after the War, its design was deemed too restless in the smaller sizes, and a revised version was cut. By that time the taste for blackletter types had subsided, even in Germany where they remained in favor into the 1940s. Gilgengart was followed by a calligraphic roman called Novalis that was cut in one size, but not issued, in deference to a more useful roman type, the seminal Palatino design of 1948. It would be hard to overemphasize the significance of this type in the history of twentieth century alphabet design. Its roots are clearly calligraphic (as its name, an homage to the sixteenth

Jan van Krimpen. Roman capitals with decorative flourishes. Hand lettering for book jacket. J. W. F. Werumeus Buning. Verzamelde gedichten. Em. Querido, 1941. 8.75 x 5.75 inches.

century Italian calligrapher Giovanbattista Palatino, attests). Its forms have distinctive, recognizable elements revealing the personality of its designer, yet it is a font in the classical vein. Details such as the elegant tapering of the main strokes, the open counters, and consummate draftsmanship are all elements of Zapf's style. Palatino proved to be eminently useful for a wide range of purposes, from modern display advertising to elegant bookwork. Unlike Van Krimpen's types, which were appreciated by a relatively small group of informed typographers, Palatino has enjoyed phenomenal success across a wide spectrum, including discerning practitioners of the typographic arts. Other popular Zapf type designs followed: the elegant titling fonts Michelangelo and Sistina; the newspaper type Melior; the innovative sans serif Optima; the phototypes Zapf Chancery and Renaissance Roman, and Zapfino, his latest font. Zapfino takes advantage of the flexibility of digital typesetting, which allows for overlapping of characters and a large character set with numerous alternate forms. These are a few among many others, each an aesthetic and popular success.

It is hard for us working in the graphic arts today to imagine a time when typeface design was dominated by engineers and mechanical draftsmen, but indeed in the early twentieth century men such as Morris Fuller Benton at American Type Founders, F. H. Pierpont at the British Monotype Corporation, and Edward E. Bartlett at Linotype were the major forces in type design. Morison, Van Krimpen, Goudy, Dwiggins, Koch, and others were pioneers in restoring the connection between calligraphy and type design; a movement that has come to full fruition in the work of Hermann Zapf, Gudrun Zapf von Hesse, and others active today. And we must not forget that, with respect to calligraphy, design, and fine printing, the groundwork for their achievements was laid even earlier, starting with the efforts of William Morris, Edward Johnston, T. J. Cobden-Sanderson, and Rudolf von Larisch.

Today we can see the influence of calligraphy in the work of some of the finest type designers. The aesthetic marriage of calligraphy and typography, so successfully integrated in the work of Hermann Zapf and Gudrun Zapf von Hesse, is also evident in the types of

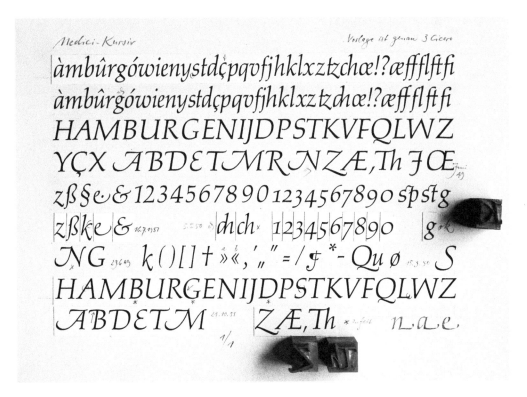

Hermann Zapf. Palatino Italic. Original working drawing for the punchcutter in 36 point. Mounted on the drawing for comparison are smoke prints of the pilot size cut by hand by August Rosenberger, also in 36 point, with metal type letters. The type was originally named Medici. Frankfurt, 1949.

Robert Slimbach (see, for example, his Minion and Poetica), Jovica Veljović of Yugoslavia and Germany (Ex Ponto, Esprit), Julian Waters (Waters Titling), and others.

Let us hope that the connection between calligraphy and typography will not again be severed, since both arts must be alive in order for each to find new expression. As T. J. Cobden-Sanderson wrote a century ago: "The printer carried into type the tradition of the calligrapher and the calligrapher at his best. As this tradition died out in the distance, the craft of the printer declined. It is the function of the calligrapher to revive and restore the craft of the printer to its original purity of intention and accomplishment. The printer must at the same time be a calligrapher, or in touch with him, and there must be in association with the printing press a scriptorium where beautiful writing may be practiced and the art of letter-designing kept alive."

This exhibition is a testament to the vitality of calligraphy and type design, and the phenomenal example and influence of Gudrun and Hermann Zapf.

Initial for Gilgengart Fraktur. Cut by August Rosenberger 1954

ABCDEFG
HIJKLLM
NOPQRST
UVWXYZ
AÖÜ

Hermann Zapf. Gilgengart Fraktur Initials. The final drawing for the punchcutter. Frankfurt, 1939.

Let us then go back to the sources of the scribe's art for new inspirations, the beautiful majuscule letters of classical Rome, for our capitals, and for our lower-case letters to the fine book-hands that by the eleventh and twelfth centuries had

ABCDEFGHIKLMNOPQRSTUVWXYZ

gradually evolved into fixed forms from the Carolingian minuscules of the ninth; not indeed to copy those forms, but to

ABCDEFGHIJKLMNOPQRSTUVWXYZ

make of them a starting point for new expressions suited to present day needs. Too many types in use today betray the

ABCDEFGHIKLMNOPQRSTUVWXYZ

fact that their designers were not conversant with the early forms of letters, that they had a feeble invention, a weak

ABCDEFGHIKLMNOPQRSTUVWXYZ

sense of proportion or propriety. Eccentricity of form from the hand of an artist who is master of himself and of his subject may be pleasing; it becomes only mere affectation when attempted by the ignorant amateur. *Frederic W. Goudy*

Hermann Zapf. Page design from *Manuale Typographicum*. Progressive weight increase in the Palatino type family: Michelangelo, Palatino, Sistina and Palatino Bold. Quotation by Frederic W. Goudy. 1954. 9 x 12.5 inches.

FAVORITE
BIBLE
VERSES
*Words of Wisdom,
Strength
and Praise*

Selected by Kitty McDonald Clevenger

Calligraphy by Hermann Zapf

♛ HALLMARK EDITIONS

Calligraphy and book design by Hermann Zapf. *Favorite Bible Verses: Words of Wisdom, Strength and Praise.* Selected by Kitty McDonald Clevenger. Hallmark Cards, Inc., Kansas City, Missouri, 1974. Text set in Crown Roman. Illustrated are the title page with facing quotation from Psalm 118, and page 24 with facing quotation from Psalm 121. 7.75 x 9.5 inches.

THE LORD IS MY SHEPHERD
The Lord is my shepherd; I shall not want.

He maketh me to lie down in green pastures: he leadeth me beside the still waters.

He restoreth my soul: he leadeth me in the paths of righteousness for his name's sake.

Yea, though I walk through the valley of the shadow of death, I will fear no evil: for thou art with me; thy rod and thy staff they comfort me.

Thou preparest a table before me in the presence of mine enemies: thou anointest my head with oil; my cup runneth over.

Surely goodness and mercy shall follow me all the days of my life: and I will dwell in the house of the Lord for ever.   *Psalm 23*

JOY COMETH
...Weeping may endure for a night, but joy cometh in the morning.   *Psalm 30:5*

24

Between 1967 and 1972, most of the alphabets designed by Hermann Zapf, and the only one designed by Gudrun Zapf von Hesse, were the result of a consulting agreement Hermann had with Hallmark Cards in Kansas City, Missouri. Since all of these alphabets were proprietary – and remain so – they are not as well known as the Zapf's other designs. Nevertheless, after three decades, they remain a significant example of how calligraphy can bring fresh inspiration to contemporary type design.

As a consultant from 1966 to 1973, Hermann's activities included annual visits, lectures and demonstrations. During that time and for some years after, Hallmark made available to interested parties a short film, "The Art of Hermann Zapf,"* and three separate exhibitions of his work "in an effort to stimulate interest, enthusiasm and appreciation in the fields of typography, calligraphy and type design." This supportive gesture, more often reserved for the "fine arts," seems remarkable even today.

Providing inspiration was also part of Hermann's role within Hallmark, especially as it pertained to the instruction of lettering and calligraphy. This resulted in a short series of instructional films and the never-published *Hallmark Lettering Instruction Manual,* which provided "new training methods, unusual tricks and time-saving techniques"– close enough to paradise for this aspiring designer and calligrapher. Alas, the *Manual* was in the mock up stage when I first saw it, and there it remains.

The beginning of the Hallmark-Zapf relationship roughly coincided with the beginning of the corporation's in-house photocomposition service, as well as the inception of its own font development group (led for close to thirty years by Myron McVay, it was where I first began at Hallmark). Though not without its technical challenges, designing for photocomposition allowed some flexibility for the designer of fonts, especially compared to traditional metal typefounding. Thus, Hallmark's first explorations into the realm of photocomposition provided Hermann an opportunity and focused time to explore new ideas, mostly for display faces, based on calligraphic forms.

As Hermann's fondness for flowers is well known, perhaps a garden analogy would be appropriate here. There is a belief by some that of the several ways to lay out a garden, the best way is to get a gardener.

*Now available on the Linotype Zapfino CD-ROM.

Hermann Zapf. Still photograph taken during the production of the Hallmark Cards film "The Art of Hermann Zapf," a film on the purpose and techniques of calligraphy. 1968.

Hallmark founder, J. C. Hall, clearly subscribed to that belief. In his never ending quest for "the very best," Mr. Hall often consulted in the early stages of corporate enterprises – and beyond – with such like-minded visionaries as Henry Dreyfuss, Walt Disney and Alexander Girard. Certainly the typographic terrain at Hallmark was worthy of a "master gardener." A business whose editorial content largely deals with human relationships must be concerned with the way in which it is presented. And no one was more committed to the desired quality than Hermann. In fact, it was, as Jeannette Lee, former vice president of the Creative organization, once told me, "the quality and refined good taste" of Hermann that attracted Mr. Hall to him. Still, it is important to note that the humanistic warmth inherent in the calligraphic line was not an especially easy sell. Engravers at Hallmark were particularly concerned that cutting letters with irregular edges would reflect badly on their reputation.

Seen together, the collection of alphabets Hermann designed for Hallmark does indeed feature essential elements of a successful garden: perspective, texture, variety. There are four perennials in the group, contemporary interpretations of important historical hands: Crown Roman (and Italic), Hallmark Uncial, Hallmark Textura and Firenze, a chancery italic with swash characters and a companion set of roman capitals named Arno. With these designs Hermann led artists on a kind of meandering walking tour through the history of written letters. Of course, this was not

A new printing type has a long, often thorny way to completion...Important in

Lectorem Delectando Pariterque Monendo
FIRENZI

the matter is the type's design; a long time is needed to perfect all its details.

Lectorem Delectando Pariterque Monendo
HALLMARK UNCIAL

The imaginary notion of letters from A to Z does not itself suffice, and by the

Lectorem Delectando Pariterque Monendo
JEANNETTE

time these more or less vague proposals and fancies attain a definite form,

Lectorem Delectando Pariterque Monendo
CHARLEMAGNE

all may look quite different on printed paper. A design needs not just any forms,

Lectorem Delectando Pariterque Monendo
SHAKESPEARE ITALIC

but good forms that harmonize with the remaining shapes, all distinguishable

Lectorem Delectando Pariterque Monendo
CROWN ROMAN WITH SWASH CAPITALS

as signs and of noble character. In addition come technical considerations that

Lectorem Delectando Pariterque Monendo
HALLMARK TEXTURA

must be thought through. Many a letter seems to strain against a form it dislikes.

Lectorem Delectando Pariterque Monendo
SCRIPTURA

Alas! it is tamed. Ever and anew it undergoes revision in black and white until it willingly accommodates itself to the higher conformity of the type fount.

Lectorem Delectando Pariterque Monendo
<small>WINCHESTER</small>

What designer in the development of his drawing does not know those spooky,

LECTOREM DELECTANDO PARITERQUE MONENDO
<small>ARNO WITH FIRENZI CAPITALS</small>

stubborn antipathetic shapes that, maverick-like, will not join the type family?

Lectorem Delectando Pariterque Monendo
<small>CROWN ITALIC</small>

They still dream of the freedom of their revered ancestors in the older scripts

Lectorem Delectando Pariterque Monendo
<small>STRATFORD</small>

whose sweeps knew no trammels... At last, after long toil, the design shows all

Lectorem Delectando Pariterque Monendo
<small>MISSOURI</small>

the characters ranged bravely and amicably together, and full of pride in his

Lectorem Delectando Pariterque Monendo
<small>SHAKESPEARE</small>

handiwork the designer delivers his work to the type-foundry....

from *About Alphabets,
Some marginal notes on type design
by Hermann Zapf,* MIT Press, 1970
Set in Crown Roman

A sampling of calligraphic fonts designed for Hallmark by Hermann & Gudrun Zapf

necessarily his plan, nor was he given total freedom, so it was an incomplete history and the reason the path was indirect. Still, there was much to be learned on the journey. A walkway that meanders allows the traveler to slow down and so better enjoy the experience. I have found that to be typical of Hermann: *delectando pariterque monendo* (by giving pleasure and at the same time instruction). Hermann planted the seeds. It was up to us to cultivate them.

Along this pathway of influential models he added three fonts that are particularly rich and unique to his œuvre: Jeannette, a rough-edged script inspired by the handwriting of Jeannette Lee; Scriptura, a rather light and airy, elegant script; and the exquisitely personal Missouri, an exotic upright italic with civilité characteristics. These three alphabets could not have been more varied from one another and so they added, to an already abundant supply, even more examples from which to study. One can almost imagine, to borrow a phrase by Warren Chappell (referring to drawing), that a feeling had gone up Hermann's arm as well as down while he was working on these. There is a quiet sense of investigation and of delight in the certainty of his own hand. After more than twenty years of designing type informed by his calligraphy (including, of course, some of the most important typefaces of the twentieth century), Hermann was in a position, professionally speaking, to fully exploit the broad-edged pen as a more determined partner with technology in the making of fonts.

The last original contribution to this distinguished collection of alphabets was Shakespeare. Designed by Gudrun, it is a simple roman spiritually related to Diotima, and equally revealing of Gudrun's refined sensibility.

At this point, the lessons illustrating the vast possibilities of calligraphy and how important it could be to alphabet design were complete. And one might assume the tour was as well. But there were still a few surprises. Three to be exact. Three additions to this already impressive array. Of course, one had to be willing to crawl through the hedgerow to find them, to a private garden Hermann and Gudrun were willing to share with those who were willing to pay attention. If, as ikebana master Bokuyo Takeda stated, "correct handling of flowers refines the personality," then the remaining lessons Hermann and Gudrun had for us began the process – while at the same time illustrating the extraordinary affinity their work has.

First there is Charlemagne (not to be confused with Carol Twombly's font of the same name), which mixes the lowercase of Shakespeare with the capital letters from Hallmark Uncial. Then Stratford, combining

Hermann Zapf. Still photograph taken during the production of the Hallmark Cards film "The Art of Hermann Zapf," a film on the purpose and techniques of calligraphy. 1968.

Shakespeare capitals with the lowercase of Hallmark Textura. And finally, Winchester, the result of combining the small capital letters of Hallmark Uncial with the lowercase letters of Hallmark Textura.

Thus, the tour was over. The only things denied were the lessons learned from seeing how Hermann might have applied this collection of calligraphic fonts. Few designers have used Hermann's types with the distinction he has. As it stands, there are just two modest examples. Both of them are small-format books stemming from Hallmark's initial venture into publishing. *Thy Sweet Love Remembered*, a collection of Shakespeare's sonnets illustrated by Bill Greer, is a two-colored jewel imbued with an elegance more commonly found in fine press books. Hermann used a small size of Gudrun's Shakespeare with generous leading, in essence allowing space to heighten the effect of each venerable line. It was one of the AIGA's Fifty Books of 1968. The second book (which I was fortunate enough to assist him with) is *Favorite Bible Verses: Words of Wisdom, Strength and Praise*. The main text, set in Crown Roman, is periodically interrupted with twelve calligraphic plates by Hermann – each a perfectly realized integration of universal words and symbols.

The Alphabet, flourishing for centuries in splendid reconciliation of science and art, possesses a power that may be revealed in part to anyone with sufficient patience and understanding. But it takes the heart and hand of a master to bring forth its noblest qualities. More than thirty years ago – when this initial educational tour began – it was the privilege of a handful of people at Hallmark to be associated with and to learn from not just one, but two such masters.

SONNET XXIX

When in disgrace with fortune and men's eyes,

I all alone beweep my outcast state,

And trouble deaf heaven with my bootless cries,

And look upon myself, and curse my fate,

Wishing me like to one more rich in hope,

Featured like him, like him with friends possess'd,

Desiring this man's art and that man's scope,

With what I most enjoy contented least;

Yet in these thoughts myself almost despising,

Haply I think on thee, and then my state,

Like to the lark at break of day arising

From sullen earth, sings hymns at heaven's gate;

For thy sweet love remember'd such wealth brings

That then I scorn to change my state with kings.

14

SONNET XXX

When to the sessions of sweet silent thought

I summon up remembrance of things past,

I sigh the lack of many a thing I sought,

And with old woes new wail my dear time's waste:

Then can I drown an eye, unused to flow,

For precious friends hid in death's dateless night,

And weep afresh love's long since cancell'd woe,

And moan the expense of many a vanish'd sight:

Then can I grieve at grievances foregone,

And heavily from woe to woe tell o'er

The sad account of fore-bemoaned moan,

Which I new pay as if not paid before.

But if the while I think on thee, dear friend,

All losses are restored and sorrows end.

15

Book design by Hermann Zapf. *Thy Sweet Love Remembered: The Most Beautiful Love Poems and Sonnets of William Shakespeare.* Selected and arranged by Dorothy Price with drawings by Bill Greer. Hallmark Cards, Inc., Kansas City, Missouri. 1968. Illustrated are Sonnets 29 and 30. First appearance of Gudrun Zapf von Hesse's Shakespeare Roman. 7.75 x 9.5 inches.

Gudrun Zapf von Hesse.
Watercolor alphabet design for poster.
24.25 x 5 inches.

Gudrun Zapf von Hesse — Bookbinding, Calligraphy and Type Design: Remarks and Musings About My Design Process

In 1991 Gudrun Zapf von Hesse was chosen to receive the Frederic W. Goudy Award from the Rochester Institute of Technology in Rochester, New York. According to Dr. Mark F. Guldin, Melbert B. Cary, Jr., Professor in Graphic Arts, the prize is awarded to designers and typophiles "who had that thread of attachment to Frederic W. Goudy, those who worked with the design of typefaces and those who have produced designs cradled in the traditional values of Gutenberg, Jenson, Aldus, Baskerville and Bodoni." Established in 1968, the first recipient of the award was Hermann Zapf. The following text is excerpted from an acceptance address presented by Gudrun Zapf von Hesse.

A few words first about my background. Some of my ancestors had early connections with type founding. They were the owners of the Luther type foundry in Frankfurt during the seventeenth and eighteenth centuries, and were in fact the successors of the famous Egenolff type foundry established in the sixteenth century. The building that housed the foundry was called Haus zum Frosch, House of the Frog. There, in 1940, type historian Gustav Mori established the German Type Foundry Museum. Unfortunately, the building was completely destroyed by air raids during World War II.

The Luther type foundry had several connections with America. The foundry delivered types to many American printing offices, especially to Christopher Sauer in Germantown, Pennsylvania. In 1743 Sauer printed the first Bible in a European language in America; the language was German. There were also close connections between the owner of the foundry, Dr. Ehrenfried Luther, and the diplomat Benjamin Franklin. In 1768 when Franklin visited Frankfurt he was a guest of the Luthers.

But I learned all this history after I had designed my first type for the D. Stempel AG type foundry in Frankfurt. I went through all the stages of type design during the past decades, and in my opinion, the best foundation for creating new alphabets is an intensive study of calligraphy.

I started practicing calligraphy when I took up the study of bookbinding in Weimar from 1934 to 1937. One afternoon a week we had to write very simple letters. I was not satisfied with this form of instruction; therefore, I taught myself at home, from a detailed examination of the works of Rudolf Koch and Edward Johnston. I carried out additional studies in 1941 with Johannes Boehland at the Berlin Graphic Arts School.

Coincidentally, my husband did his first exercises in letterforms in his hometown of Nuremberg at the same time. He also used the same instructional books by Johnston and Koch.

After the war, in 1946, I moved to Frankfurt to start my own bindery. I got permission to do my bindings on the premises of the Bauer type foundry. At the Bauer foundry I began my first connection with type and the art of punchcutting. It was fascinating to watch the punchcutters, and one day I asked if I could try to cut a punch by myself. I did quite a good job and eventually I cut a complete alphabet in brass, which I named Hesse-Antiqua, for use in gold tooling of bindings. In addition I also made decorating tools under the guidance of Joseph Spahn, the chief punchcutter at the Bauer type foundry. To everyone's regret the Bauer foundry was closed in 1972, ending a great tradition in German type production.

From 1946 until 1954 I was a calligraphy instructor at the Staedel Art School in Frankfurt. The calligraphy that I did in the 1940s in Frankfurt, especially the texts of "Hyperion to Diotima" by Friedrich Hölderlin, was the source for the typeface Diotima, issued in 1951.

I started creating alphabet designs to be used for photocomposition many years later. A private commission from Hallmark Cards resulted in the typeface Shakespeare, first issued for a Hallmark publication of Shakespeare's Sonnets in 1968. At that time all the letters of Shakespeare Roman and Italic had to be fixed within an 18-unit system, and for the manufacturing of the grids the drawings needed to be very precise.

We had a lot of problems in the early years of photocomposition. Take my Diotima types, transferred into film by Linotype/Stempel and Berthold. The delicate hairlines so beautifully executed for letterpress printing by August Rosenberger came out much too thin in photocomposition. You can't print such a version on coated or smooth paper – the type misses the ink spread of letterpress printing, which Rosenberger had taken into account when cutting the punches for metal type. But I was never consulted when the Diotima types were redesigned for photocomposition by the design departments of the companies. I saw the results after everything was finished. It was too late to start over again and change the concept completely. There was a big loss in appearance of this Diotima version in comparison to the original letterpress type.

Today, bold versions of alphabets are needed. I was not so happy about the creation of a Heavy Diotima.

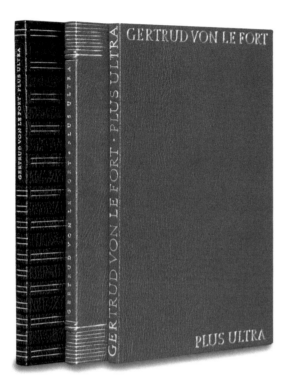

Bookbindings by Gudrun Zapf von Hesse. *Plus Ultra,* by
Gertrud von Le Fort. Morocco leather, hand tooled in gold.

Gudrun Zapf von Hesse. Hand lettering, personal mono-
gram for use as logotype on exhibition brochure. 1998.

As you know, Diotima is the name of a Greek priestess
in Plato's dialogue about love, and I think in the philos-
opher's imagination she had to be slim and beautiful.
But, in any case, I showed the designs of the bolder
version of Diotima to Günter Gerhard Lange of
Berthold. We decided not to follow the basic Diotima
designs, and in the end a complete new alphabet for
photocomposition was developed, called Nofret
(the Beauty). It was named after the Egyptian queen
Nofretete (Nefertiti), and was released by Berthold in
1987. Nofret was designed as a text face, but with
small caps and different weights it can be used also in
display and job work. Alex Osborn's *Your Creative
Power* was the first book that I saw printed in this type.
It was designed by Hayward Blake and published by
Motorola University Press. It is beautifully done in
every detail, using Nofret Roman and Italic, and for
emphasis, the bold versions. This book was shown in
my exhibition at the Cary Library at the Rochester
Institute of Technology (RIT) held in 1991.

More recently I have produced several new types
for digital composition. I designed Carmina for
Bitstream Inc., in Cambridge, Massachusetts. I had to
draw the light and heavy versions for the roman and
the italic; the other weights for digital systems were
executed by means of a computer assisted drawing
system called Ikarus. Like the Nofret design this face
has four weights.

My three newest type designs were displayed for
the first time at the RIT exhibition; it always takes
years to get everything finished. Christiana was designed for Berthold in Berlin. The drawings were done
in 1989 and the type was released in 1991. Colombine,
a connected script alphabet, was designed for Unter-
nehmensberatung Karow Rubow Weber GmbH
(URW) in Hamburg. This alphabet is based on my
handwriting. It was done especially for the Signus
system of URW – a computer based drawing system
for headlines. It is also used for signage production
with a kerning program and the ability to modify.

Alcuin, my newest alphabet was also designed for
URW Hamburg. Alcuin was the advisor to Charlemagne, born in England circa 735 and died in Tours,
France, in 804. Under his guidance the reform of letterforms took place. The Carolingian minuscule was the
result. This letterform has been a favorite of mine for
many years, and I preferred this style in my examples
written with a broad-edged pen. At one time I started
experimenting with letterforms for a typeface in this
classic Carolingian – of course it should not be an historic copy, but an interpretation to be transformed into
a type of our day. Alcuin with its strong calligraphic
expression may be used in books, magazines, and also

in the area of printed office communications.

How types are used and for what purpose are always out of the control of the designer. Designers usually don't have any influence as to how their typefaces are composed, spaced, or modified – with more or less taste – in advertisements, books, magazines, and commercial printing.

When I look around our house in Darmstadt I see examples of my calligraphy and bookbinding everywhere: alphabet combinations cut in black paper; ornamental arrangements of letters in watercolors; Renaissance sonnets written in German together with the original texts in Spanish, French, and Italian; calligraphic letters written with a broad-edged pen; examples of hand bindings for special editions; bindings for manuscripts written by my husband; hand-cut tools used for bindings; quotations hand tooled in gold, and my own logo.

In contrast, the new electronic tools now in the hands of type designers may save a lot of time during the preparation of the drawings, but there is the danger of the loss of the human touch which is so very necessary for a good type. I think it is important and good news that these days people are again interested in the use of calligraphy to influence the type design of the future.

I would like to thank you for choosing me to receive the 1991 Frederic W. Goudy Award. It is really the coronation of my professional life. I am very proud to be included in the list of distinguished people in the graphic arts who have received this award. Perhaps my husband, Hermann Zapf, now fears a little that I will go on strike for cooking and housekeeping. But joking apart he is delighted too.

You decided to give the Frederic W. Goudy Award for the second time to a woman. The first was given in 1980 to Edna Beilenson in New York. Many times women have influenced the lives of printers and artists. Edna Beilenson was very closely connected with the books that Peter Beilenson printed at the Peter Pauper Press. She was one of the great personalities in the graphic arts. We all know the important role that Bertha Goudy played in the life and work of Frederic W. Goudy. In the painting by Tom Fost in the School of Printing at RIT you can see Frederic working on his types and you see Bertha in the background with the composing stick in her hand: two people engaged so closely in the graphic arts during their lifetime. At home in Darmstadt my husband and I have a different situation. Hermann and I are in a more competitive situation and normally we are not working together.

It was in the 1970s, in the first years of digital type design, that I helped him to prepare bitmaps by hand

Type specimen sheet for Smaragd, a display typeface of roman capitals with figures, released by D. Stempel AG in 1954. The American name for the type is Emerald, an English translation of the German name. 11.75 x 8.25 inches. See catalogue entry 78, page 77.

Gudrun Zapf von Hesse. New Year's greeting, 1987. Pencil drawing of roman majuscule letterforms. 8.25 x 4 inches.

for his alphabet designs Marconi and Edison, for Dr. Ing. Rudolf Hell GmbH in Kiel. We used preprinted black grids and with white color took away the pixels to shape the letters. It was hard work and in this case I had more patience than Hermann. Therefore, I had to help him again in preparing a special alphabet for the *World Book Encyclopedia* in Chicago. These bitmap designs were such an unusual load of work, and we had such a short deadline, that he really did need my assistance.

We each have our own studio in our home, separated by the biggest possible distance. Each of us does his or her own work and is completely independent. Only to make critical remarks do we look at the other's work. It is not easy for me to compare with Hermann. His work is so perfect from the first moment; whereas I need much more time before I am really satisfied. Besides the design work, Hermann is responsible for our garden. He loves to work in the garden and my responsibility is of course the function of the household.

You may be interested in how we got together. This happened in Frankfurt in 1948. Hermann was art director of the D. Stempel AG typefoundry. I moved to Frankfurt after the war in 1946. My home town is Potsdam, near Berlin. After the war Potsdam was under Russian occupation, and therefore, it was not a good place at all to start a new life.

Hermann visited an exhibition of my calligraphy in Frankfurt with a director of the Stempel foundry, Dr. Lepold. They liked my letterforms and I was invited to their office for a meeting.

This was my start in type design. But it was also the start of some disputes with this young art director,

Hermann Zapf by name. After the first letters of the Diotima were cut by the punchcutter August Rosenberger, Hermann wanted the roman much more condensed compared to my original design. We exchanged our arguments and once a day I said to him, "Herr Zapf, is it your typeface or my design?" He never will forget this. As usual in life we ended up in a compromise. The type was executed a bit condensed. We met halfway. But I confess the narrower version of the Roman was good for the type, especially to be used as a text face.

August Rosenberger was really a great master. He cut the pilot size of Diotima in 36 point. I wanted as much as possible to keep the calligraphic touch in my letterforms, the lively contour of the drawings that I had done on a mouldmade paper with a rough surface. My thanks to August Rosenberger for he kept the personal expression so beautifully in this typeface. But unfortunately you can see this only in the metal type, not in the versions of Diotima in done for photocomposition years later.

The first publication set in Diotima was *Plus Ultra* by Gertrud von le Fort in 1953. It was selected for the German Fifty Books in 1954. Gotthard de Beauclair did the typography and I did the bindings using my own handmade paste paper. Diotima Roman was released in 1951 and a companion Diotima Italic in 1953. Also in 1953 Rosenberger cut the display face Ariadne Initials, an all-caps alphabet. Smaragd (Emerald) was released by Stempel in 1954. The Smaragd type was used with the Diotima Italic in a presentation to Hermann Hesse when he received the "Friedenspreis" from the

German Book Trade in 1955. All these typeface designs were made for metal type.

The fighting with Hermann for the best and ideal form went on over some time. At the end the best solution in such a situation was to marry each other. This took place in August 1951. After forty years I think it was a very good decision.

My connections with the Stempel foundry strengthened after I opened a bookbinding studio in their building in 1948. It was extremely difficult to find a place in the heavily bombed city of Frankfurt so soon after the war. But the Stempel foundry was interested in special bindings for publications printed by their private printing office which was under the direction of Hermann at this time. My studio was on the next floor, and with one apprentice I started my bindery.

In my bindings I like the flexible method with thin boards and very small borders. This was contrary to the method I was taught during my apprenticeship from 1934 to 1937. I learned bookbinding in the studio of Professor Otto Dorfner in Weimar, which had also been the bindery for Count Harry Kessler of the famous Cranach Press. In 1940 I received the master diploma. In the following years I developed my own style, very simple and pure in decoration, carefully executed in every detail. The flexible binding was becoming my specialty.

My bindery was closed in 1955. Our son Christian, born that year, needed all my time. You can't do bindings next to the cradle and then run into the kitchen to prepare meals to feed your people. To do good bindings you must concentrate completely on your job. But in my heart I am still a little sorry about having had no time in all those years to do some bookbinding.

In life you have to make compromises, and you have to make decisions to go in one or the other direction. After the years passed I was able to concentrate more of my time again on calligraphy and type design.

I have had many commissions for alphabet design. First in the art of metal type and then in the last decades for photocomposition and digital systems. I personally still like the old method of designing my basic alphabets by hand, for I want not to be dominated by a computer. Hermann played with one of the very first Macintosh computers, which he received as a gift from Steve Jobs. Hermann got some gray hairs from making experimental designs on the Mac. Since that time, I think he has never trusted a personal computer.

Everyone must find his or her own method in designing alphabets. My recommendation for young designers would be to train your hand and sharpen your eyes in the study of historic letterforms; together with a calligraphic background, the art of alphabet design will survive.

Ein wichtiger Punkt der Lebensweisheit
besteht in dem richtigen Verhältnis,
in welchem wir unsere Aufmerksamkeit
teils der Gegenwart, teils der Zukunft widmen,
damit nicht die eine uns die andere verderbe.

Viele leben zu sehr in der Gegenwart:
Die Leichtsinnigen.
Andere zu sehr in der Zukunft:
Die Ängstlichen und Besorgten.

ARTHUR SCHOPENHAUER

Gudrun Zapf von Hesse. New Year's greeting, 1993. Pen calligraphy, Carolingian minuscule. Quotation by Arthur Schopenhauer. 8 x 5.25 inches.

Palatino väterlich gewichtig und namensgleich mit dem italienischen Schreibmeister des 16. Jahrhunderts, bestimmt die Schrift-Familie, welche unter der Bezeichnung Palatino zusammengefaßt ist. Lebendig, als eine typische Kursiv, steht daneben die *Palatino-Kursiv* Für die Linotype gibt es dazu eine identische Kursiv und Halbfette in den Werkschriftgraden. Die **Halbfette Palatino** ein robustes Familienmitglied, ist nützlich überall, wo es gilt, eine Titelzeile durchzusetzen oder eine Anzeige lautstark zu machen. Anmutig zeigen sich die PALATINO-KAPITÄLCHEN in Kapitelüberschriften. *Schwungfiguren* zur Palatino-Kursiv dagegen sind vorwiegend im Akzidenzbereich verwendbar, wo ihr graziöses und bisweilen kapriziöses Wesen begrüßt wird. Bei Arbeiten, wo eine monumentale Wirkung erstrebt wird, ist die MICHELANGELO willkommen. Versalien dieser Art sind von zeitloser Gültigkeit, ernsthaft und festlich zugleich. Die stattlich wirkende Schwester **SISTINA** vermag sich mit ihrer kräftigeren Stimme auch im Marktwirbel der lauten Akzidenzschriften zu behaupten. PHIDIAS {ΦΕΙΔΙΑΣ} der griechische Vetter der Michelangelo, zeigt die geistige Verwandschaft des Griechischen mit dem Römischen. Auch die **Heraklit** (Ἡρακλειτου) als griechische Auszeichnungsschrift paßt gut zur Palatino. Ein wichtiger Zweig innerhalb der Palatino-Familie ist die Linotype-Aldus-Buchschrift *mit Kursiv*, und neuerdings die Enge Linotype Aldus-Antiqua *mit Kursiv*, welche überall als Werkschriften die Palatino ergänzen, wo ein leichteres und schmaleres Buchstabenbild erforderlich ist. Nicht vergessen den kraftvollen Schwager **Kompakt** denn er bewältigt oft die schwierigsten Probleme, ohne dabei plump oder derb vorzugehen. Den lieblichsten Kontrast dazu bilden die zarte *Virtuosa I & II* zwei Schwestern, die eine stiller, die andere bewegter im Ausdruck. Die griechische Kusine dieser Virtuosa-Schwestern *Frederika (Φρειδερίκης)* steht an Liebreiz ihren Verwandten nicht nach. Kein Familienjubiläum, kein Geburtstag ohne die SAPHIR stets ist der Entwerfer beglückt von ihren festlichen Buchstaben. Schließlich sei die Frakturschrift Gilgengart nicht vergessen. Zwar gehört sie zum deutschen Schriftzweig, neben mancher Type der Palatino-Familie steht sie aber so gut, daß man sie gern zur Verwandten ernennen möchte.

Hermann Zapf   Back to the Sources:
Some Reflections on Calligraphic Types

When printing with movable type was invented by Johannes Gutenberg in the middle of the fifteenth century, the handwritten letter was the source for the design and cutting of typefaces. Gutenberg used the textura of the medieval scribes for printing his 42-line Bible in Mainz in 1455. The first roman letters were cut by Adolf Rusch in Strasbourg in 1464, who was followed one year later by Sweynheim and Pannartz in Subiaco, near Rome. Their roman types followed the forms of the handwriting of the humanists.

In the following centuries we observe a gradual degeneration as type design moved away from the written model to more monotone letters, culminating in the sans serif and slab serif designs created at the beginning of the nineteenth century. Through the years roman letters became over-sharpened with very thin hairlines.

The lifeless interpretation of roman types changed in 1889 with William Morris and his Golden type design. He tried to go back to the sources of the fifteenth century. Morris wanted to return the human hand to type design. With the Golden type he started the revival of type design. The calligraphic influence can also be seen in Bruce Rogers's design for his Centaur type of 1914. He used photographic enlargements of a roman alphabet cut in 1476 by Nicolas Jenson in Venice. For the drawings to be given to the punchcutter he used a broad-edged pen, writing over gray enlargements of Jenson's characters.

In the years after William Morris, type foundries commissioned artists to design new typefaces. At the beginning of the twentieth century it was mainly the Klingspor typefoundry in Offenbach that did this. Rudolf Koch designed many alphabets for the Klingspor foundry, and the broad-edged pen was his tool for the drawings. In this connection other type designers must be mentioned: F. H. Ernst Schneidler, who worked for the Bauer foundry in Frankfurt, and Georg Trump, whose types were released by C. E. Weber in Stuttgart. But all these typefaces were cast in lead and only a few are available for digital resolution today.

Facing page, left. Hermann Zapf. Variation of a title page for the Palatino type family, designed for the Stempel typefoundry, Frankfurt am Main, 1960. A descriptive text serves as a background on which variations of the Palatino family are displayed, supplemented by other Zapf typefaces which can be used with them. From *Typographic Variations.* Museum Books, New York, 1964. 12 x 8 inches.

On the other hand, there is an increasing demand in recent years for types with a calligraphic touch. We see a strong tendency towards more personal alphabet designs based on calligraphy. After the sans serif period of the 1960s and 1970s, dominated by Helvetica, we notice that people got tired of the uniform and cool appearance of typography seen everywhere. As at the end of the nineteenth century, more personal expression is wanted now.

Many types with a calligraphic appearance were discovered again when calligraphers worldwide had a chance to show their talents through photocomposition. The many technical restrictions of casting processes for metal types could be completely ignored. But even so, in the era of photocomposition the designer was still not independent from technical limitations. As a designer I am not happy with my design of ITC Chancery, which I did in 1977 for the International Typeface Corporation (ITC) in New York. The characters lack the elegance of written forms. Producing alphabets in the early years of photocomposition meant compromise: the letters had to be squeezed into a 21-unit system, conforming to the standards of the time. The hairlines had to be thickened to meet the needs of special, but primitive, photocomposing equipment. ITC Chancery should be redesigned in the direction it was originally conceived, with thin hairlines, and the various letters should be connected.

The new digital technology presents ideal conditions to retain the calligraphic structure of a design. Today we are able, through digital technology, to completely realize our intentions, in every detail. In discovering the versatility of computers we have gained possibilities we never had before, and of which we could not even dream only a few years ago. Calligraphy is again the basis for new type designs, as it was at the beginning of the era of movable type. Designers have a wide field in which to use their imaginations, to serve the type market in the future. This exhibition in the San Francisco Public Library shows many examples of type designs connected to calligraphy, connected with the human hand.

A selection of my type designs, as well as designs by my wife Gudrun Zapf von Hesse, are displayed in the exhibition. Shown, with an emphasis on written forms, are my Optima, Hunt Roman, Civilité, Euler, Renaissance Antiqua and Zapfino. From my wife are the following alphabets: Hesse Antiqua, Diotima, Ariadne Initials, Smaragd, Alcuin, Nofret and

Colombine. In addition the work of fourteen other type designers is exhibited: Alan Blackman, Erik van Blokland, Rick Cusick, Timothy Donaldson, Jean Evans, Phill Grimshaw, Cynthia Hollandsworth, Akira Kobayashi, Richard Lipton, Jacqueline Sakwa, Robert Slimbach, Viktor Solt-Bittner, Jovica Veljović and Julian Waters.

Optima, next to Palatino, is my most successful typeface. The design started in 1950 and the type was released by the D. Stempel AG typefoundry in conjunction with Linotype GmbH in Frankfurt. I made the very first sketches for a roman letter without serifs in Italy. After a visit to Santa Croce in Florence, in October 1950, I drew some marble intarsia letters that I saw on grave plates in the church. As, at that moment, I had no other paper with me, I used two 1000 lire bank notes. These letters on the floor at Santa Croce inspired me to use the principle of roman letters without serifs for a typeface.

To be observed on one of the 1000 lire notes are two names for a typeface: Fiorentina and Firenze. Later I changed the name to Neu-Antiqua, as one can see marked on the original drawings made for the punchcutter August Rosenberger at the Stempel foundry. All of these names are much better than the final name "Optima Roman," decided on by the sales people of the D. Stempel AG typefoundry in Frankfurt. Even the internal name by the foundry employees – Metro – was better.

The letters of Optima are designed in the proportions of the Golden ratio, with an x-height of 1:5, and of 1:3 for the ascenders and descenders. The typeface has been used in many ways and for many purposes. One prominent example of the use of Optima is the display of 58,220 names of American soldiers, inscribed in black granite, at the Vietnam Veterans Memorial in Washington, D.C., designed by Maya Lin in 1982.

Hunt Roman is a private typeface, commissioned in 1961 by the late Mrs. Rachel McMasters Hunt, for the use of the Hunt Botanical Library in Pittsburgh, Pennsylvania. In collaboration with Jack Stauffacher, who was then head of the New Laboratory Press at the Carnegie Institute of Technology in Pittsburgh, a design was developed for headings and displays, to be

Hermann Zapf. Page design from *Manuale Typographicum.* Asymmetric grouping of two typefaces: Michelangelo and Palatino Italic. 1954. 9 x 12.25 inches.

Hermann Zapf. Lao-tzu's eighty-first sentence from the Tao-Te Ching: "Truthful words are not beautiful. Beautiful words are not truthful. Good men do not argue. Those who argue are not good. Those who know are not learned. The learned do not know." Silkscreen print, three colors on gold leaf. 1971. 16.25 x 16.25 inches.

ABC
DEFGHIJKLM
NOPQRS
TUVW
XYZ

I consider

the variety of humors among men,

and despair of pleasing everybody;

ABCDEFGHIJKL
MNOPQ
RSTUV
WXY
&Z

yet I shall not therefore leave off printing.

ABCDEFGHI
JKL
MNOPQR
STUVW
XYZ

I shall continue my business.

I shall not burn my press

and melt my letters.

ABCDEF
GHIJKLM
NOPQR
STU
VWXYZ

ABC
DEFGHIJKLMN
OPQRSTUVWXYZ

Benjamin Franklin

An Apology for Printers

Hermann Zapf. Quotation by Benjamin Franklin. Leaf from *Orbis Typographicus: Thoughts, Words and Phrases on the Arts and Sciences.* Experimental typography designed by Hermann Zapf. Quotation set in Codex. Capitals clockwise from upper right corner: Open Kapitalen, Fry's Ornamented, Smaragd, Romanée Titling, Hadriano Stone Cut. 1980. 12 x 9 inches.

composed in conjunction with Jan van Krimpen's Monotype Spectrum. The type was cut in steel at the D. Stempel AG typefoundry in Frankfurt, in 1962. Unfortunately an italic font was never cut. The type is exclusively used in America by Davis & Warde, Inc., Pittsburgh, and by Jack Stauffacher at The Greenwood Press in San Francisco.

Civilité was the idea of Paul H. Duensing, who had a private typefoundry in Kalamazoo, Michigan. He saw a page in my publication *Pen and Graver,* which I had designed during the War in the years 1939 through 1941. These alphabets and pages of calligraphy were cut by hand on lead plates by August Rosenberger. In 1971, after studying my other sketches and propos- als for swash characters, Paul H. Duensing engraved the mats in brass in 1971 for the casting. The type is now produced by the Harold Berliner Typefoundry in Nevada City, California. Two of the most beautiful publications printed in Zapf Civilité are *The Devil's Thoughts* by Samuel Taylor Coleridge (Kelly/Winterton

Press, 1989), and Leonard Baskin's *Zapf's Civilité Disclosed,* which shows typographic examples, pro- duced at his Gehenna Press in Leeds, Massachusetts, in 1995.

Euler is a type family for printing mathematics. Generally mathematics are printed from types made by punchcutters in the eighteenth and nineteenth centuries. The Greek letters of those types, especially, had no characteristic elements remaining from the forms originally written by hand. Various recuttings of the Greek and mathematical characters led to the interpretations of today. In 1979, Donald E. Knuth of the Department of Computer Science at Stanford University had the courage to propose a completely new design to bring new blood into the printing of mathematics. From the beginning, the design of the different new alphabets of roman, Greek, cursive and fraktur was supported by several American universi- ties, working together with Knuth and the American Mathematical Society in Providence, Rhode Island.

The typeface was released in 1983, and was named in honor of Leonhard Euler (1707–1783), a Swiss mathematician who lived and worked primarily in St. Petersburg, Russia.

Knuth's concept for the design of Euler was to move away from the ordinary looking alphabets for mathematics. Several mathematical formulas and notes by famous mathematicians like Euler and Einstein were studied. We wanted to bring back into the letterforms the handwritten character created by the stroke of the quill, as in the past.

The Euler project archive in the Green Library at Stanford University contains all the correspondence, drawings, proofs and computer printouts associated with the design. The digitization of Euler was done by Carol Twombly and Dan Mills using the Metafont program developed by Knuth at Stanford.

My Renaissance Antiqua design was begun in 1984. It resulted however, from one of my early designs: Palatino (released in 1950). The success of Palatino resulted from the personal touch in the letterforms. Small irregularities, arising from the execution of the letters by hand, gave the Palatino alphabets a warm expression. The basic handwritten elements were not removed but were carefully preserved by the punchcutter August Rosenberger. Later, because of the photocomposition manufacturing process, these were gradually lost. Unfortunately I was not always consulted and the manufacturers' excuse was that such designs had to be quickly produced to satisfy their customers' needs.

The wide popularity of Palatino also had a negative side: it is the most copied typeface in the world. In the absence of copyright controls, there is no way to prevent the distribution and sale of the many pseudo-Palatino alphabets now on the market, with their primitive designs. I am blamed because everyone thinks that what he or she bought is my original design, since a similar sounding name is often used.

Unauthorized digital copies of Palatino are offered for sale, with obscure labels, but people can get authentic Palatino alphabets through Linotype Library GmbH and Microsoft Corporation. Their digital version in OpenType consists of four alphabets, each containing over 1,200 characters. The roman, italic, bold and bold italic have more than 4,800 characters in total, including all the various accented letters and special characters for all the languages using the Latin, Greek and Cyrillic alphabets.

In 1984, to avoid a digital copy of Palatino, I proposed a new interpretation to Scangraphic Dr. Böger GmbH in Hamburg, Germany. This was the reason Zapf Renaissance Antiqua was developed. It was a

Hermann Zapf. Kalender 2001: Grafische Werkstatt für Technik & Kunst, Offenbach am Main. Poster combining Zapfino alphabets with a design set in Michelangelo from *Manuale Typographicum II.* 19.25 x 13.5 inches.

welcome opportunity to take advantage of digital resolution (Palatino was originally developed as a hot-metal typeface). Unlike Palatino, Renaissance Antiqua was conceived as a true type family and has a range of weights including a light, book and a bold version with italics. In addition, small caps and, for the first time, italic small caps were offered, plus many extra characters, ligatures, swash characters and finials. The typeface was released in 1985.

Zapfino started out as a script face, not to compete with handwritten forms or as a copy of calligraphy. You can't get the life and freshness of a broad-edged pen with a machine. But Zapfino may compete with the many badly designed calligraphic alphabets that have infected the PC and Macintosh market since the 1990s. It should be considered an alphabet opposing bad taste in digital alphabet design.

The work on Zapfino started in California in 1993. David Siegel at Stanford proposed the development of an unusual script typeface to be generated by a sophisticated typographic computer program. This attracted my interest. Several problems in the execution delayed the project, and after five years it was released by Linotype Library GmbH in Bad Homburg, Germany, in a simplified arrangement of four alphabets combined with many ligatures, extra long descenders, and one hundred ornaments and signs.

Many script alphabets have already been designed. To start the new Zapfino alphabet I went back to a calligraphic example, a quotation by Hans von Weber that I remembered having done in one of my sketch-books during the War, when I served in a geographic unit in Bordeaux, France. I had written out this text with a pointed Sommerville pen. In all the years of metal type and photocomposition it was impossible to use these letterforms as a basis for an alphabet design, as they were highly sloped and the letters overlapped. But these limitations do not matter when designing for digital composition.

The more lively expression found in types that come out of the stroke of a broad-edged pen has had its influence on typography in the past decades. Even new sans serif alphabets are moving away from the abstract rules underlying Paul Renner's Futura and Max Miedinger's Helvetica designs. The coolness in typographic interpretation has been replaced by a more human style.

In the coming years the design of types will remain an interesting subject for designers, independent of the method of designing a new alphabet. You may prefer to draw or write the characters by hand – as I do, for I like to use my hands – or you may take a PC or Macintosh as your tool and transfer the forms to the computer with a scanner, making corrections directly on the screen.

Let us hope that alphabets based on truly new ideas will be offered to the type market in the future. In past years we have seen that market inflated by designs of questionable originality. There is always a need for good designs as an expression of the time in which we live, and as our contribution to the world of books, magazines, and advertising.

The Exhibition

Neue Alphabete können nur eine logische
Weiterentwicklung bereits bestehender Schriftformen sein,
entworfen für die heutigen Setz- und Drucktechniken
und als ein Ausdruck der Zeit, in der wir leben.
Der automatisierte Photosatz von morgen
wird bis in alle Einzelheiten durchdachte
Entwurfs-Systeme erfordern
und wir werden werkgerechte Lösungen nur erarbeiten,
wenn wir uns von überholten Formen
der Vergangenheit lossagen.
Die Welt verändert sich heute schneller
als in früheren Jahrzehnten.
In dieser Welt stellt das gedruckte Wort
einen gewaltigen Machteinfluss dar.
Die Druckindustrie vermag
ebenso wie die anderen Massenmedien
– Radio und Fernsehen – täglich Millionen
von Menschen zu beeinflussen.
Sie sollte sich dieser Verantwortung
stets bewusst sein.

Hermann Zapf

ABC
DEFGHIJK
LMNOP
QRSTUVW
XYZ

New alphabets
can only be
a logical evolution
of letterforms already existing,
designed for modern techniques
of composition and as an expression of our own time.
Tomorrow's computerized photo-composition developments
will demand new design systems prepared to the last detail,
and we shall devise working solutions only
if we dissociate ourselves from the outdated forms of the past.
The world today changes more swiftly than it did in former decades.
In this world the printed word
will be an influence of tremendous power.
And since the printing industry, like the other mass media
– radio and television – can influence millions of people daily,
it must remain fully aware of its responsibility.

abcdefghijklmnopqrstuvwxyz

Hermann Zapf

The work of Hermann Zapf needs little introduction to typographers and calligraphers. Zapf may be the most significant and successful type designer of the twentieth century. He is certainly one of the most prolific, with nearly 200 designs to his credit. Among calligraphers, his name is identified with letterforms of superlative grace and near perfection, arranged in designs that are at once vital, dynamic and sophisticated. Zapf's work has long been held as a standard by which the contributions of others in both fields are measured.

Typography was born in the world of the scribes, but it gradually grew away from its origins, and by our own time had become something that had little to do with calligraphic tradition. Hermann Zapf has changed that. He has succeeded in making the skill and knowledge of the calligrapher once again important in the creation of new designs for typefaces. This was not only because of his premier calligraphic talent, but also because of his unflagging pursuit of new methods and technologies for the production of type. His designs have spanned all the industries concerned with type manufacture, from hand punchcutting and metal typecasting, through photocomposition and today's digital technology.

Although he is rooted in the best calligraphic and typographic traditions, Zapf's enthusiastic search for new methods has continued to this day. For example, his latest major design, the script family Zapfino, was released in 1998, the year Zapf turned 80. It is the result of years of effort to create a calligraphic type that is free of the constraints imposed by metal typefounding and photocomposition. The four Zapfino alphabets incorporate many variations and special characters heretofore only available to the calligrapher. They are intended to be typeset harmoniously with overlapping flourishes, ascenders and descenders.

Born November 8, 1918 in Nuremberg, Germany, Zapf wanted to become an engineer. Political conditions in Germany in the 1930s prevented this, and because his artistic talents were obvious, he apprenticed as a photographic retoucher. He taught himself calligraphy and lettering by studying the books of Rudolf Koch and Edward Johnston, and began freelancing as a lettering artist in 1938.

Facing page, left: Quotation by Hermann Zapf from *Manuale Typographicum.* Z-Presse, Frankfurt am Main, New York, 1968. Set in Optima and Optima Semibold. 12 x 8.25 inches. See catalogue entry 9, page 50.

During World War II, Zapf was conscripted into the army and was stationed in Bordeaux, France, where he served in a cartographic unit. After the war, in 1947, he became art director of the D. Stempel AG typefoundry in Frankfurt am Main. In 1948, he began to teach lettering at the Werkkunstschule in Offenbach. In addition, he started to design books for such publishers as Suhrkamp and S. Fischer. He also began designing the first of many successful typefaces.

His first typeface, Gilgengart, is a fraktur designed between 1938 and 1941. It was followed by the roman types Novalis, Palatino, Michelangelo and Melior. Other types followed throughout the 1950s, including Sistina, Virtuosa, Sapphire, Aldus, Heraklit Greek, Kompakt, Alahram Arabic and others. Optima, the very successful sans serif, was issued near the close of the decade following the war, in 1958.

In the 1950s Zapf also began his long association with the typesetting industry and allied enterprises in the United States. He worked as a consultant to the Mergenthaler Linotype Company in Brooklyn and Berlin from 1956 to 1974, and in 1960 taught graphic design at the Carnegie Institute of Technology in Pittsburgh, Pennsylvania. His association with Jack Stauffacher at the Carnegie Institute resulted in the development of Hunt Roman in 1963. From 1969 to 1972 Zapf consulted for Hallmark Cards in Kansas City, Missouri, for whom he designed a number of calligraphic typefaces, including Crown Roman, Jeanette Script, Firenze, Hallmark Textura, Hallmark Uncial, Winchester, Charlemagne, Stratford, Missouri, Scriptura, and Arno.

Many other notable designs followed in the 1960s and 1970s. These include Medici, Orion, Marconi, Zapf Civilité, Noris Script, Comenius, Zapf Book (in four weights), Zapf Dingbats, and Zapf Chancery.

Hermann Zapf has addressed the needs of the contemporary designer by creating type families, with various weights of letterforms, to provide a range of weight and style choices within one unified type design. In the 1980s his designs included the mathematical typeface Euler, Aurelia, Pan Nigerian, Zapf Renaissance, URW Roman and URW Sans Serif

Throughout his career Zapf has enlarged the usefulness of his designs by creating new fonts of his existing faces, for example, adding Greek character fonts to the already existing Optima. More recently, he has expanded his Palatino design for use on desktop computer systems. Each Palatino style now has more than 1,200 characters.

Hermann Zapf has also been active in the area of fine printing and publishing. He has written, produced, or been the subject of a number of books featuring his calligraphy, typography and type design. These are consistently of the highest quality, bringing together all that is best in the bookmaking arts. Their titles include *Das Blumen-ABC* (1948), *Feder und Stichel* (1949) (published in English as *Pen and Graver* in 1952), *Manuale Typographicum I* (1948–1950), *Manuale Typographicum II* (1968), *Typographic Variations* (1963), *About Alphabets* (1960), *Orbis Typographicus* (1980), *Poetry through Typography* (1984), *Ein Arbeitsbericht*

(1984), *Hermann Zapf and His Design Philosophy* (1987), *ABC-XYZapf* (1989), and others.

Zapf also has long experience as a teacher of typography and lettering. From 1972 to 1981 he taught these subjects at the Technische Hochschule in Darmstadt, Germany. He was a professor of typographic computer programming at the Rochester Institute of Technology in Rochester, New York, from 1977 to 1987, where he also taught calligraphy courses. He has written two instructional books on calligraphy and was featured in a demonstration film on his calligraphic technique, produced by Hallmark Cards, Inc.

Honored with many prizes and awards, he was the first recipient of the F. W. Goudy Award from the Rochester Institute of Technology, in 1969. In 1974 he was the recipient of the Mainz Gutenberg Prize, and was made an Honorary Royal Designer for Industry by the Royal Society of Arts in London in 1985. In 1989 he was awarded a gold medal at the international book exhibition in Leipzig. More recently, in 2001, he was awarded a Lifetime Achievement Award by the Friends of Calligraphy, San Francisco, California.

In bringing type design back to its fundamental source – calligraphy – Hermann Zapf has proved that the work of the hand is the creative power behind the throne of technology.

Florenz
Santa Croce
Oktober 1950

2

OPTIMA

1   Optima type specimen sheet.
    Type specimen sheet, including Optima Italic and
    Optima Bold. Not dated. 7.25 x 9.25 inches.

→ 2   Drawing of Santa Croce, Florence, Italy.
    Pencil drawing showing church façade. Underneath the
    drawing of the church are sketches, also in pencil, of
    letters observed on pavement of the church floor. Blue
    ballpoint pen sketches of first trial letters in the style of
    Optima Roman are drawn lengthwise along the right
    side of the sheet. October 1950. 8 x 5.75 inches.

Firenze, Dom-Museum (Opera di S. Maria del Fiore)

Aus dem oberen Fries der Kanzel mit dem Psalm Davids.

MPⱯDNŁ

Sängerkanzel (früher im Dom)

von Luca della Robbia 1431–1438

OTER

Firenze, Santa Croce

Chiostro di S. Croce, Capella Vieri- Canigiani

(Ancona d'Altare in terra invetriata) Della Robbia

NAPQKFC

Battistero di S. Giovanni

Tomba dell Anipapa Giovanni XXIII (1421–1427) · Donatello » Fede, Speranza e Carità « (Michelozzo)

(Glaube, Hoffnung und Liebe)

Z 2·10·1950

3

→ 3 Drawing of Renaissance letters.
Ink drawings of fifteenth century intarsia letters observed in the Cathedral Museum and on pavement in Santa Croce church, Florence, Italy. Hermann Zapf's notations are written in pencil. October 2, 1950. 8.25 x 11 inches.

→ 4 Italian banknotes with drawings of letters.
Two 1000 lire banknotes showing the first sketches for the typeface Optima, based on Hermann Zapf's direct observation of fifteenth century inscription letters in Santa Croce church, Florence, Italy. Banknotes were used because, at the time, Zapf was carrying no other paper for sketching. On one of the banknotes is Zapf's first idea to name the type Fiorentina or Firenze. October 3, 1950. 3 x 6.25 inches.

OPTIMA

ABCDEFGHIJKLMNOP
QRSTUVWXYZ
abcdefghijklmnopqrst
uvwxyz
12345 & 67890

Philosophie der Neuzeit
STOCKHOLM
Klassische Dichtung

SCHRIFTGIESSEREI D. STEMPEL AG FRANKFURT AM MAIN

8

5   Cover of Optima Antiqua type specimen book.
    Optima Antiqua, Eine Original-Schrift von Hermann Zapf.
    D. Stempel AG, Frankfurt am Main, 1958. The Optima
    type specimen book, issued by the D. Stempel AG
    typefoundry. Printed by the foundry's in-house
    printing office. 11.75 x 8.25 inches.

6   Page from Optima Antiqua type specimen book.
    The first page of the book describing the history and
    development of the typeface. Reproduced is a sketch of
    inscription letters, made in Rome by Hermann Zapf.
    1958. 11.75 x 8.25 inches.

7   Page from Optima Antiqua type specimen book.
    The second page describing the structure of the type.
    Illustrated with sketches from Santa Croce, Florence, Italy,
    made in 1950 by Hermann Zapf. 1958. 11.75 x 8.25 inches.

→ 8   Optima type specimen sheet.
    Type specimen sheet, issued by D. Stempel AG, showing
    alternate designs for the capital letters M and N. Not dated.
    11 x 8 inches.

9   Leaf from *Manuale Typographicum.*
    One leaf (page 85) from a special unbound copy of
    Manuale Typographicum. By Hermann Zapf. Z-Presse,
    Frankfurt am Main, New York, 1968. Set in Optima and
    Optima Semibold. 12 x 8.25 inches. Illustrated on
    page 44.

10 Leaf from *Manuale Typographicum.*
    One leaf (page 87) from a special unbound copy of
    Manuale Typographicum. By Hermann Zapf. Z-Presse,
    Frankfurt am Main, New York, 1968. Set in Optima
    Roman in two sizes. 12 x 8.25 inches.

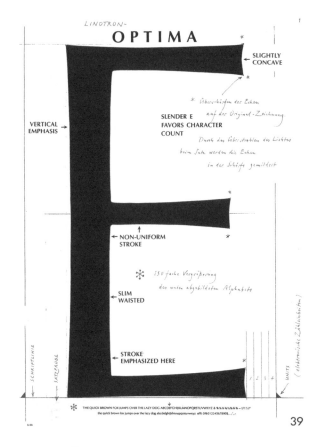

11

13

→ 11   Enlargement of Optima Roman E.
Letter E showing the slightly curved lines of the stem of
Optima Roman. This enlargement is made from Linofilm
Optima and illustrates the overly sharpened corners
necessary for phototypesetting equipment in the 1960s.
Not dated. 10.75 x 8 inches.

12   Proof sheet for Optima Medium.
First proof of 10 point Optima Medium, issued by D.
Stempel AG. The text, by Hermann Zapf, on the design
of new printing types. Today the Optima type family
consists of twelve styles and weights. February 1967.
11.75 x 8.25 inches.

→ 13   Photograph of Vietnam Veterans Memorial,
Washington, D.C.
The memorial, designed by Maya Ying Lin, was opened
in 1982. Optima was chosen for the inscription of 58,220
names on the black granite wall. Photograph by Ann
Hawkins, Washington, D.C. Not dated. 11.75 x 8 inches.

14   Page opening from *About Alphabets*.
About Alphabets: Some Marginal Notes on Type Design.
By Hermann Zapf. Typophiles, New York, 1960. Pages 38
and 39. The main text is set with wide interlinear spacing.
The more closely set lines are a commentary on the main
text. Set in Optima Roman. 7.25 x 4.5 inches.

17

18

HUNT ROMAN

15 Page opening from *Hunt Roman: The Birth of a Type*.
Hunt Roman: The Birth of a Type. Commentary and Notes by
Hermann Zapf and Jack Werner Stauffacher. Pittsburgh
Bibliophiles, Pittsburgh, Pennsylvania, 1965. An illustrated
narrative on the design and production of Hunt Roman.
On the first page of his commentary, Hermann Zapf
recounts the initial conception for this typeface, designed
and produced for the exclusive use of the Hunt Botanical
Library. Book design by Jack Stauffacher, set in Hunt
Roman and Monotype Spectrum. 7 x 9.25 inches.

16 Page opening from *Hunt Roman: The Birth of a Type*.
Hunt Roman: The Birth of a Type. Commentary and Notes by
Hermann Zapf and Jack Werner Stauffacher. Pittsburgh
Bibliophiles, Pittsburgh, Pennsylvania, 1965. At the end
of his commentary Hermann Zapf pays tribute to Jack
Stauffacher, who was instrumental in arranging the
commission and production of the type. The page is faced
with a foldout illustration of the first proof of the 18 point
pilot size of Hunt Roman. 7.25 x 9.75 inches.

→ 17 Reproduction of calligraphic broadside;
drawing for Hunt Roman Italic.
"Song" by William Shakespeare, written out by Hermann
Zapf in 1960 for Paul Standard, New York. This calligraphy
was the source of the design for Hunt Roman. Below the
roman script is a 1971 proposal for an italic version, which
was never cut as type. 9 x 6 inches.

→ 18 Rough sketches and early drafts for Hunt Roman.
Hunt Roman was commissioned by Rachel McMasters
Miller Hunt on behalf of the Hunt Botanical Library,
Carnegie Institute of Technology, Pittsburgh, Pennsylvania.
The lower portion of the page shows working drawings
for the alphabet, rejected by Hermann Zapf as too narrow.
October 1961. 11.75 x 8.25 inches

19 Proof sheet of 14 point Z-Antiqua [Hunt Roman].
Z-Antiqua was the in-house name used by D. Stempel AG
for Hunt Roman. Foundry proof sheet printed on Japanese
paper. December 14, 1962. 11.75 x 8.25 inches.

Hermann Zapf · October / November 1961

âbçdefghijklmñ
⁎   ⁎   ⁎

opqrstúvwxyz
⁎   ⁎

ABÇDEFGHIJK

LMNÒPQRST

ÜVWXYZ&ÆŒ

¶æœffffl.,:;!?Th

$1234567890¢

seperate → | á | ← cut here

← base line

← descender line

⁎ *the lower-case letters* aeonu
*will also cast on a smaller body
to add the different accents.
(only a third of the letters)*

20

→ 20 Drawing of Hunt Roman, for the punchcutter.
Drawing prepared for the punchcutting department at
D. Stempel AG, with annotation for the special casting
of accented letters. October–November 1961.
14.75 x 10.5 inches.

DECALOGUE FOR CRAFTSMEN
by Porter Garnett of the Laboratory Press

1 Thou shalt not imitate.

2 Thou shalt not cater.

3 Thou shalt not seek effectiveness for its own sake.

4 Thou shalt not seek novelty for its own sake.

5 Thou shalt not employ expedients.

6 Thou shalt not exploit thyself nor suffer thyself
   to be exploited by others.

7 Thou shalt not concern thyself with the opinions
   of any but the sensitive and the informed.

8 Thou shalt not give to anyone the thing that
   he wants, unless for thyself the thing that he
   wants is right.

9 Thou shalt not compromise with popular taste
   nor with fashion nor with machinery
   nor with the desire of gain.

10 Thou shalt not be satisfied — ever.

Printed at the New Laboratory Press, College of Fine Arts, Carnegie Institute of Technology.
Handset in Hunt Roman, a type designed by Hermann Zapf. 18 June 1963

23

21 Leaf from *Manuale Typographicum.*
   One leaf (page 99) from a special unbound copy of
   Manuale Typographicum. By Hermann Zapf. Z-Presse,
   Frankfurt am Main, New York, 1968. Text by Jack
   Stauffacher. Set in Hunt Roman. 12 x 8.25 inches.

22 Typographic broadside, The New Laboratory Press.
   Printing specimen from the New Laboratory Press,
   quotation by Porter Garnett. Designed and printed by
   Jack Stauffacher for the fiftieth anniversary of the
   Book Club of California. Hermann Zapf designed the
   pressmark. Set in Hunt Roman. 1962. 13 x 9.5 inches.

→ 23 Typographic broadside, *Decalogue for Craftsmen.*
   Quotation by Porter Garnett of the Laboratory Press.
   Broadside designed and printed by Jack Stauffacher at
   the New Laboratory Press. 1963. 12.75 x 9.25 inches.

24 Page opening for a booklet.
   An excerpt from the text of a lecture by Albert Camus,
   "Create Dangerously" (1957). Handset in 14 point Hunt
   Roman. Designed and printed by Jack Stauffacher at the
   New Laboratory Press, May 1963. 13 x 9.5 inches.

Civilité

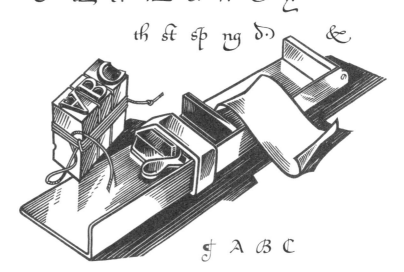

ʃ a b b c d d e f g g h i j k l l m

n o p qu r s t u v w x y z

z

& a. t. n. e. r. y.

th ſt ſp ng d.

ʃ A B C

D E F G H I J K L M N O

P Q R S T U V W X Y Z

& A B D D E H I K

1983   L P R S V ? !

» $ 1 2 , 3 4 5 , 6 7 8 . 9 0 ¢ «

25

ZAPF CIVILITÉ

Nürnberg, den 17. Juli 1940

26

→ 26 Calligraphic civilité characters.
       Pen written civilité characters with flourishes, prepared
       as a study for a calligraphic manuscript. Nuremberg,
       July 17, 1940. 5.75 x 8.75 inches.

→ 27 Leaf from *Pen and Graver*.
       Calligraphic civilité alphabet. Page 22 from *Pen and Graver.
       Alphabets and Pages of Calligraphy.* By Hermann Zapf; preface
       by Paul Standard; cut in metal by August Rosenberger.
       Museum Books, New York, 1952. The design and cutting
       of the plates were done during wartime, from 1939 to
       1941. 8.5 x 11.75 inches.

→ 28 Leaf from *Pen and Graver*.
       Calligraphic civilité script. Page 23 of *Pen and Graver.
       Alphabets and Pages of Calligraphy.* By Hermann Zapf; preface
       by Paul Standard; cut in metal by August Rosenberger.
       Museum Books, New York, 1952. Quotation by
       Giambattista Bodoni, "Letterforms gain in grace when not
       written uneasily nor belabored with mere skill, but rather
       with delight and love." 8.5 x 11.75 inches.

ABC
DEFGHIKLMNOP
PQRSTUVWXYZ

aabcdvefghiklmnopqrſtuvwxyz

27

Die Buchstaben haben dann Anmut,
wenn sie nicht mit Unluſt und Haſt,
auch nicht mit Mühe und Fleiß, ſondern
mit Luſt und Liebe geſchrieben ſind

BODONI

28

31

29 Reproduction of first sketches for Zapf Civilité.
    Broad-edged pen calligraphy by Hermann Zapf, 1971,
    for his civilité type. Published in a special section in
    Fine Print: The Review for the Arts of the Book 11, no. 1
    (January 1985). 11.75 x 8.75 inches.

30 Reproduction of two pages from *Pen and Graver*.
    Pencil drawings of additional civilité characters added by
    Hermann Zapf to printed pages of his *Pen and Graver* in
    1971. Published in a special section in *Fine Print: The Review
    for the Arts of the Book* 11; no. 1 (January 1985).
    11.75 x 8.75 inches.

→ 31 Final drawing for Zapf Civilité.
    The final drawing of the civilité alphabet, annotated by
    Hermann Zapf, for cutting the metal type matrices. The
    matrices were cut by Paul H. Duensing, a private type
    founder in Vicksburg, Michigan. 1971. 11.75 x 8.25 inches.

32 Foundry proof for Zapf Civilité.
    The foundry proof, printed by Paul H. Duensing, showing
    the character set included in one font. Not dated.
    9.75 x 8 inches.

VI

He saw a cottage with a double coach-house,
A cottage of gentility;
And the Devil did grin, for his darling sin
Is pride that apes humility.

VII

He peeped into a rich bookseller's shop,
Quoth he! we are both of one college!
For I sate myself, like a cormorant, once
Hard by the tree of knowledge.

VIII

Down the river did glide, with wind & tide,
A pig with vast celerity;
And the Devil looked wise as he saw how
      the while, It cut its own throat.
»There!« quoth he with a smile,

35

33 Proof sheet for Zapf Civilité.
    The first proof sheet, printed by Paul H. Duensing, for
    checking distances between letters. Not dated.
    9.75 x 6.75 inches.

34 Prospectus for Zapf Civilité with sample metal types.
    Type prospectus issued by Harold Berliner's Typefoundry
    in Nevada City, California. The type was cast by Harold
    Berliner from matrices cut by Paul H. Duensing. Not
    dated. 11 x 8.5 inches.

→ 35 Page opening from *The Devil's Thoughts*.
    The Devil's Thoughts. By Samuel Taylor Coleridge.
    Kelly/Winterton Press, New York, 1989. Typography and
    hand printing by Jerry Kelly, for an edition of sixty copies.
    Set in Zapf Civilité. 12.75 x 8.5 inches.

abcdefghijklmnopqrstuv

wxyz1234567890074fj

ABCDEGHIJLMNOP

QRSTUVWXYZKKFT

αβγδεζηθικλμνξοπρσς,

τυφχψω1234567890φ

ΓΔΘΛΞΠΣΦΨΩΛΞΨ

Hermann Zapf · July/August 1980

36

ℵ 𝔑 𝓕 𝓡 B N A P U R — U A A Y S ?

AMS - EULER

1752048639 1372549ό = + ← [{ (

ΠΓΔΘΥΩΞΛΦΨ **ΛΘΣΓΦΩ** ζξ

CZFSLNQBWIXKYHTI E=mc²

First sketches

37

EULER

Hermann Zapf '80

Aleph

38

EULER

→ 36 Drawing for Euler.
Roman and Greek characters. Mathematics typeface based on an idea by Professor Donald E. Knuth, Department of Computer Science, Stanford University. Developed for the American Mathematical Society, Providence, Rhode Island. July–August 1980. 8.25 x 11.75 inches.

→ 37 Drawing with first sketches for Euler.
The drawing shows the pointed zero character specially designed to avoid confusion with the letter O in mathematical typography. Not dated. 4.25 x 8 inches.

→ 38 Drawing for Euler.
The first proposal for the fraktur and capital script characters. 1980. 8.25 x 11.75 inches.

39 Drawing for Euler Roman.
Large scale outline drawings for roman letters for the digitization of the type by the Department of Computer Science at Stanford. Produced with Metafont, a computer design programming system, developed by Donald E. Knuth. 1981. 7.25 x 11 inches.

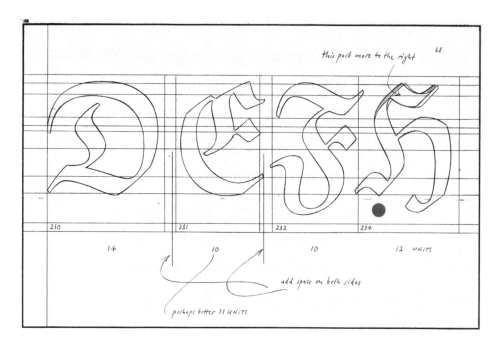

40

EXCLUSIVELY BY SCANGRAPHIC DR. BÖGER GMBH

49

ZAPF RENAISSANCE ANTIQUA

→ 49 Zapf Renaissance Antiqua specimen book.
The specimen book notes the type was issued exclusively
by Scangraphic as part of its digital type collection.
Scangraphic Dr. Bögner GmbH, Wedel bei Hamburg,
Germany. Not dated. 12.75 x 9 inches.

50 Diskette for Zapf Renaissance Bodytypes and Supertypes.
"Bodytype" is a foundry name for text settings, while
"Supertype" indicates display settings. Disk in Macintosh
Type 1 Format, from the Scangraphic Digital Type
Collection. 1994. 3.75 x 3.5 inches.

a b c d d e f g h i j k l m n o p q r s t u v w x y z ? ß

A B C D E F G H I J K L M N O P Q R S T U V W X

Y Z & 1 1. 2. 3. 4. 5. 6. 7. 8. 9. 0.

st sp th k

x   nach links
x   nach rechts in den Satzspiegel

= INSGESAMT PLUS 26 ZEICHEN

53

Zi
1970

54

64

LIG.

55

AAUP

THE ASSOCIATION OF AMERICAN UNIVERSITY PRESSES

CERTIFICATE OF AWARD

Has been selected as one of 50 books of outstanding merit in concept, design, and manufacture & will be presented in the traveling exhibit. This book demonstrates those particular qualities held intrinsic to the craft of fine bookmaking.

Awarded at the fiftieth-anniversary meeting of The Association of American University Presses, Tuscon, Arizona, June 1987, and presented to

Juror Hermann Zapf, Darmstädt

56

HERMANN ZAPF

AND HIS DESIGN PHILOSOPHY

Selected Articles and Lectures on Calligraphy
and Contemporary Developments in Type Design,
with Illustrations and Bibliographical Notes,
and a Complete List of His Typefaces

57

→ 56 Certificate for an award.
Certificate for outstanding merit in fine bookmaking;
set in Zapf Renaissance, for the Association of American
University Presses, June 1987. Zapf was juror for the
award. 8.5 x 11 inches.

→ 57 Book jacket for *Hermann Zapf and His Design Philosophy.*
Cover titling set in Zapf Renaissance. Reproduced on
the jacket is a limited edition print by Hermann Zapf of
a magic square: SATOR AREPO TENET OPERA
ROTAS. *Hermann Zapf and His Design Philosophy.* By
Hermann Zapf. Society of Typographic Arts, Chicago,
Illinois, 1987. 12 x 32.25 inches.

The claims of contemporary art cannot be ignored in any **vital scheme** of life. _____ **The art of today is that which really belongs** to us: it is our own reflection. In condemning it **we but condemn ourselves.** _____ We say that the present age possesses no art: — who is responsible for this? It is indeed a shame that despite all our rhapsodies about the ancients we pay so little attention to our own possibilities. _____ Struggling artists, weary souls lingering in the shadow of cold disdain! In our self-centered century, what inspiration do we offer them? _____ **The past may well look with pity at the poverty of our civilization; the future will laugh at the barrenness of our art.**

We are destroying art in destroying the beautiful in life.

58

→ 58 Typographic broadside, *Homage to Tokyo.*
Quotation from *The Book of Tea,* by Kakuzo Okakura.
Keepsake for the Alliance Graphique International Japan
Congress, Tokyo, May 1988. Set in Zapf Renaissance. The
Japanese *kanji* characters were written by Aita Shinohara,
Tokyo. 12.5 x 12.5 inches.

59 Page opening from *ABC-XYZapf.*
From a collection of short essays written about Hermann
Zapf by friends, students and admirers, to commemorate
his fifty years in alphabet design (pages 164-165). Half
the contributions are in German, with English synopses,
and half in English. Designed by Hermann Zapf and
illustrated with his work. Set in Zapf Renaissance.
ABC-XYZapf: Fifty Years in Alphabet Design. Edited by John
Dreyfus and Knut Ericson. Wynkyn de Worde Society,
London/Bund Deutscher Buchkünstler, Offenbach, 1989.
11 x 7.5 inches.

60

ZAPFINO

→ 60 Specimen poster for Zapfino.
The four Zapfino alphabets with a selection of some
of the one hundred ornaments that accompany the
type fonts. Published by Linotype Library GmbH, Bad
Homburg, Germany. 1998. 23.75 x 19.75 inches.

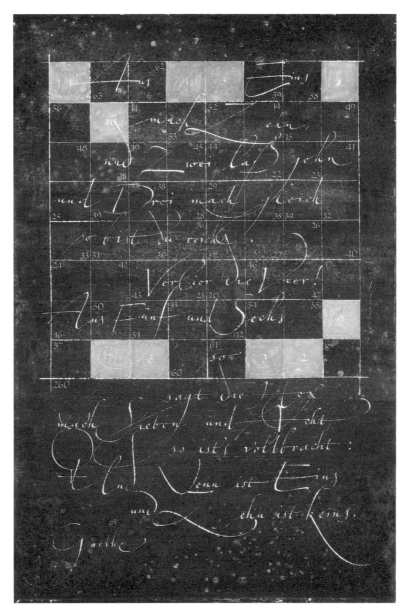

61

61 Specimen booklet for Zapfino.
    Booklet contains a history and description of the type-
    faces, with reproductions of calligraphy from Zapf's 1944
    sketchbook and a sgraffito panel of a magic square. The
    sgraffito tempera panel, selected for illustration here, is a
    quotation by Johann Wolfgang von Goethe: The Witch-
    compound from Faust, Part I, with a magic square based
    on the number 260, attributed to Mercury. 1970. Panel:
    23.5 x 16 inches. Specimen booklet by Linotype Library
    GmbH. 1998. 10 x 27.5 inches.

62 Specimen booklet for Zapfino.
    Type specimen booklet of the four Zapfino type alpha-
    bets, a selection of ornaments, and lowercase letters with
    large ascenders, descenders and swashes. Also displayed
    is a setting of a translation of the Hans von Weber text
    shown as calligraphy on the reverse side. Linotype
    Library GmbH. 1998. 10 x 27.5 inches.

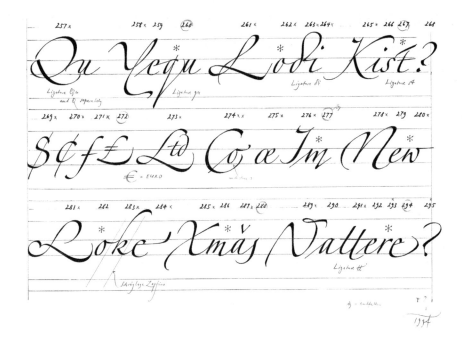

66

65

70

Wie kann man bei der Wahl schwanken,
ob man sein Leben den Frauen oder den Büchern weihen soll!
Kann man eine Frau, wenn sie ihre Launen hat,
zuklappen und ins Regal stellen?
Wanderte schon einmal ein Buch, ohne dich zu fragen,
einfach aus deinem Zimmer weg in den Bücherschrank eines anderen?
Hat je ein Buch, stand dir gerade die Lust zu einem anderen,
wolltest du schlafen oder auch nichts tun,
von dir verlangt, du solltest gerade jetzt es lesen
und ihm allein dich widmen? Werden die Suppen von Büchern versalzen?
Können Bücher schmollen, Klavier spielen?
Einen Mangel freilich haben sie: sie können nicht küssen!
Hans von Weber

63

Ariadne-Initialen

A B C
D E F G H I K L
K O N Z E R T
M N O P Q R S T
U V W X Y Z
R L V Z

SCHRIFTGIESSEREI D. STEMPEL AG FRANKFURT AM MAIN

Gudrun Zapf von Hesse

The typefaces of Gudrun Zapf von Hesse, like those of her husband Hermann Zapf, reveal a heritage of the best calligraphic traditions. Although they have often been associated with her husband's types, they naturally have their own distinct personalities, and they are perhaps best described as classic, timeless, and elegant. They demonstrate an underlying strength of form, styled with delicacy, refinement, and grace. Although she has concentrated her efforts mainly in the design of text styles, she has also designed single font calligraphic typefaces meant for display use. Her accomplishments in type design and calligraphy have been recognized with the 1991 Frederic W. Goudy Award from the Rochester Institute of Technology, and more recently in 2001 with a Lifetime Achievement Award from the Friends of Calligraphy.

Born on January 2, 1918 in Schwerin, Germany, Gudrun Zapf von Hesse began the study of calligraphy in 1934, at the same time that she began her training as a bookbinder. She took calligraphy courses and, like Hermann Zapf, independently studied the books of Rudolf Koch and Edward Johnston. In addition, she studied calligraphy with Johannes Boehland at the Berlin Graphic Arts School. Between 1934 and 1937, she trained as a hand bookbinder with Professor Otto Dorfner in Weimar, where she earned a master diploma. She then worked for a time in Berlin as a bookbinder.

Settling in Frankfurt after World War II, Gudrun Zapf von Hesse was allowed to work on the premises of the Bauer type foundry in Frankfurt to produce her bindings. There, she became interested in the art of punchcutting, eventually producing an original alphabet that she cut in brass for use in tooling gold stamped letters on bookbindings. As well as continuing to produce bookbinding commissions, she taught calligraphy at the Staedel Art School in Frankfurt from 1946 until 1954. She discontinued her bookbinding practice on the birth of her son Christian in 1955, but carried on designing type, as time and family duties permitted.

Gudrun Zapf von Hesse met Hermann Zapf in 1948, when the D. Stempel AG foundry invited her to produce the design that was to become Diotima. At the time, Hermann Zapf was the art director for the Stempel foundry, and he was responsible for overseeing the type's production. The two designers were married in 1951.

In the early 1950s, three typefaces by Gudrun Zapf von Hesse were released by the Stempel foundry: Diotima Roman and Italic, Ariadne Initials, and the titling face Smaragd. The Ariadne Initials, consisting of flourished italic capitals, reveal the direct influence of the broad-edged pen in their makeup. Their classic style permits a harmonious mixture with other types.

In 1968 she designed the typeface Shakespeare for Hallmark Cards, first used in a Hallmark publication of Shakespeare's sonnets. This design was followed by Carmina, produced for Bitsream Inc. in 1987. The Nofret type family (named for the Egyptian queen Nofretete, or Nefertiti), was designed for Berthold and was also released in 1987. Christiana, also for Berthold, appeared in 1991.

The typeface Colombine, based on Gudrun Zapf von Hesse's handwriting, was designed for URW Hamburg and released in 1991. The calligraphic roman Alcuin, also for URW Hamburg, appeared in 1992.

It is worthwhile to note that Gudrun Zapf's early types – Diotima, Ariadne Initials, and Smaragd – have been showcased to great effect by her husband Hermann Zapf in his special publications on typography and fine printing, notably in both volumes of his *Manuale Typographicum,* as well as in other books. These examples demonstrate the great adaptability of her typefaces in mixed use with other fonts. This is one characteristic, among others, that will ensure their survival in the typographic repertory.

Facing page, left: Gudrun Zapf von Hesse. Ariadne Initials type specimen sheet. Ariadne is a single alphabet of italic swash capitals designed to accompany Diotima, or for use as display type. 11.5 x 8 inches. See catalogue entry 77, page 76.

68A

72

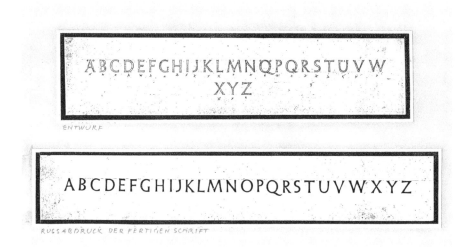

70

HESSE ANTIQUA

→ 68A Hesse Antiqua. Photograph of bookbinder's hand
lettering tools.
Unique set of brass letters, mounted on wooden handles,
for hand stamping or tooling of letters on bookbindings.
Gudrun Zapf von Hesse designed and cut in brass a single
alphabet at the Bauer type foundry, Frankfurt am Main,
in 1946–47. Close view showing details of the brass letters.
Not dated. 4 x 5.5 inches.

68B Hesse Antiqua. Photograph of bookbinder's hand
lettering tools.
Another view of the tools. Not dated. 4 x 6 inches.

69 Photograph of development of Hesse Antiqua.
The progressive stages of Hesse Antiqua, from pencil
drawings of the letters through smoke proofs of the
alphabet to a sample of the letters hand stamped in gold
on leather. Also shown is Hesse Antiqua titling on two
bookbindings by Gudrun Zapf von Hesse. Not dated.
6 x 4.5 inches.

→ 70 Drawing and smoke proof of Hesse Antiqua.
Illustration of the complete alphabet in two stages of its
development. Not dated. 8.25 x 11.75 inches.

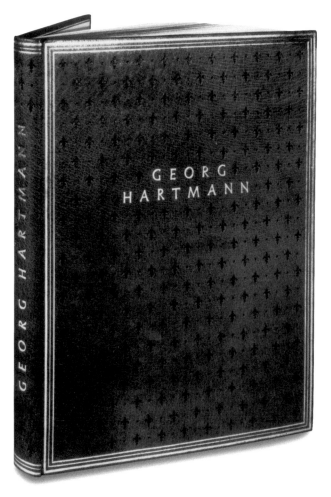

71

71 Photograph of bookbinding with titling in Hesse Antiqua.
A special publication in honor of the seventieth birthday
of Georg Hartmann, director of the Bauer typefoundry,
Frankfurt am Main. Hand bound in brown pigskin by
Gudrun Zapf von Hesse. The binding has a blind stamped
design and gold stamped titling in Hesse Antiqua. This
is the first use of the alphabet for this purpose. 1947.
10.5 x 7.75 inches.

72 Photograph of Hesse Antiqua tools, with gold stamped
vellum panels.
Hesse Antiqua hand lettering tools displayed with two
vellum panels, gold stamped by Gudrun Zapf von Hesse.
Not dated. 4 x 6 inches.

73 Photograph of gold stamped vellum panel.
Vellum panel of a text by Gerhard Marcks. The lettering,
in a free arrangement of lines, was hand stamped in gold
using Hesse Antiqua lettering tools. Not dated.
4.5 x 5.5 inches.

74 Photograph of vellum panel, *Der Nachtigallen Baum*
(The Nightingale Tree).
Vellum panel, hand stamped in gold using Hesse
Antiqua lettering tools and leaf ornaments. Not dated.
6 x 4.75 inches.

75

THE DIOTIMA TYPE FAMILY
Diotima, Smaragd, and Ariadne Initials

→ 75 Calligraphic broadside.
Handwritten broadside, ink on mold-made paper. The
text block, written out in an italic hand, is bordered
with majuscule letters written in the style of the Ariadne
Initials and shows variations in letterforms. Source of
text not identified. Not dated. 9.5 x 12.5 inches.

→ 76 Cover of type specimen book.
Diotima, Smaragd, Ariadne Initials. D. Stempel AG,
Frankfurt am Main. Diotima specimen book, printed by
the foundry's in-house printing office, including both
Diotima Roman and Diotima Italic typefaces with the
display types Ariadne Initials and Smaragd. Released by
D. Stempel AG between 1951 and 1954. Not dated.
11.75 x 8.25 inches.

77 Ariadne Initials type specimen sheet.
Initial letters developed to accompany the Diotima
typeface. The font consists of italic swash capitals only,
modeled on forms written with a broad-edged pen. The
type punches were cut by August Rosenberger, punchcutter at D. Stempel AG. The initials combine successfully
with many typefaces. Released by D. Stempel AG in 1953.
Specimen sheet not dated. 11.5 x 8 inches. Illustrated on
page 72.

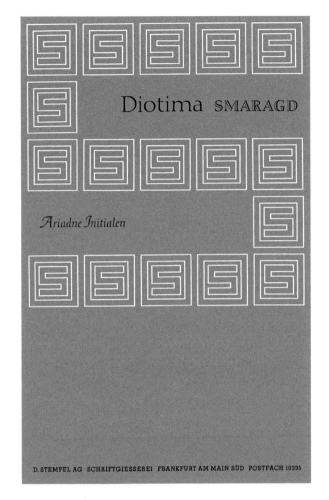

Diotima SMARAGD

Ariadne Initialen

D. STEMPEL AG SCHRIFTGIESSEREI FRANKFURT AM MAIN SÜD POSTFACH 10335

76

*Ach Bedenke
Christ Das Ende,
Fürchte Gott *
* * Harre Jn
Kindlicher Lieb, *
Murre Nicht,
* Ob Pein &
Qual Rumoren,
* *Sey Tugend-
Voll & Wandle
eXemplarisch * *
YederZeit *

um 1755
Joh. Muscat
Nürnberg

79

78 Smaragd type specimen sheet.
    Type specimen sheet for Smaragd, a display typeface of
    roman capitals with figures, released by D. Stempel AG in
    1954. The American name for the type is Emerald. Not
    dated. 11.75 x 8.25 inches. Illustrated on page 33.

→ 79 Letterpress print with text by Johann Muscat.
    Ariadne Initials combined with Diotima Italic. Each word
    in the text begins with a different letter of the alphabet,
    from A to Z. The print is designed as an alphabet
    exemplar using Ariadne Initials to begin each word.
    1955. 8.25 x 2.75 inches.

80 Page opening from *Vergil: Bucolica.*
    Vergil: Bucolica. Suhrkamp Verlag, Frankfurt am Main,
    1957. A bilingual bibliophile edition, in Latin with German
    translation by Rudolf Alexander Schröder; woodcuts by
    Aristide Maillol. Designed by Hermann Zapf and printed
    by the Max Dorn Presse, Offenbach am Main. The Latin
    text is set in Diotima Roman. The problem of the longer
    lines of German text is solved by setting them in Diotima
    Italic. 10.5 x 14 inches (page opening).

Nicht, daß irgendeine Form, irgendeine Meinung siegen wird, dies dünkt
mir nicht die wesentlichste Gabe des Frie-
dens. Aber daß der Egoismus in allen seinen Gestalten sich beugen wird unter die
heilige Herrschaft der Liebe und Güte, daß
Gemeingeist über alles in allem gehen, daß
das Herz in solchem Klima erst recht auf-
gehen und geräuschlos, wie die wachsen-
de Natur seine geheimen weitreichenden
Kräfte entfalten wird, dies mein ich, dies
seh ich und glaub ich.

FRIEDRICH HÖLDERLIN

Gudrun von Hesse 1948

81

→ 81 Calligraphic broadside with text by Friedrich Hölderlin.
Original calligraphy with text by Friedrich Hölderlin.
Ink on Ingres paper. Gudrun von Hesse was invited by
the D. Stempel AG foundry to develop the Diotima typeface based on this lettering. 1948. 17.5 x 12.5 inches.

82 Calligraphic broadside.
Original calligraphy. Roman majuscule letters written
with a broad-edged pen on Ingres paper, intended as
model drawings for the Diotima capitals. Not dated.
8.25 x 11.75 inches.

A B C D E F G H I J J K L M N Orb Pr Q
Ro S Tor Ufer Vater Wi X Y Z K Z
Æ Œ A Ö U Ç ! ? ¢ & & * (§
a b c d fg g ch i j et k o l m n p quer o s u
voll w x y z   3 4 5 6 7 8 9 0
ff fi fi fl ft ck æ œ ß ß , – - « „ ' ; ,

Godmin von Hesse
1948

83

DIOTIMA * ABC
DEFGHIJKLMNOPQRSTUVWXYZ
»abcdefghijklmnopqrstuvwxyz«
ABCDEFGHIJKLMNOPQRSTUVW
XYZ * DIOTIMA

¢ Æ Œ Ç Ø ✛ 1234567890 [1952]

84

→ 83 Calligraphic alphabet for Diotima.
The completed design for the typeface including ligatures,
figures and punctuation. Written with a broad-edged
pen. Individual letters were cut from pages of working
drawings and pasted together on a single sheet. This was
given to August Rosenberger, punchcutter at D. Stempel
AG, who cut the punches for the type directly from the
drawings. 1948. 8.25 x 11.75 inches.

→ 84 Diotima type specimen sheet.
Specimen sheet printed in black and red on Japanese
paper by the in-house printing office at D. Stempel AG,
including special characters and figures. 1952.
10.5 x 14.5 inches.

THEODOR HEUSS

dem liberalen Manne,

der ein Leben lang die Würde des Menschen vertrat,

dem großen Schriftsteller, der Vergangenheit

und Gegenwart von gefährlichen Ressentiments befreite und den

hellen und sauberen Verstand an ihre Stelle setzte,

dem redlichen Menschen,

der Anmut und Würde mit nobler Geistigkeit verband,

und der – ein Vorbild für viele in schwerer Zeit – Idee und Wirklichkeit

in seiner Person und in seinem Werk in Einklang brachte,

verleihen wir den

FRIEDENSPREIS DES DEUTSCHEN BUCHHANDELS

Frankfurt a. M., in der Paulskirche, am 11. Oktober 1959

BÖRSENVEREIN

DES DEUTSCHEN BUCHHANDELS E.V.

Vorsteher

87

85   Specimen page from Liber Librorum.
Specimen title page for the Latin Vulgate Bible, set in Diotima Roman. Liber Librorum was an international project carried out to celebrate the 500th anniversary of the Gutenburg 42-line Bible; organized by Bror Zachrisson, Stockholm and Hermann Zapf. A portfolio of typographic specimens for Bible designs was distributed by the Royal Library of Sweden. 1955. 13.25 x 9.25 inches.

86   Specimen page from Liber Librorum.
First chapters of Genesis, Latin Vulgate Bible. The body of the text is set in 12 point Diotima Roman. Included in a portfolio of typographic design specimens for the Bible created for Liber Librorum. Typographers and printers from fifteen countries took part in this international project. 1955. 13.25 x 9.25 inches.

→ 87   Certificate for an award.
Printed certificate for the Friedenspreis des Deutschen Buchhandels, designed using Diotima Roman. The name of the recipient, Theodor Heuss, who was President of the German Federal Republic, is set in 36 point capital letters and printed in color. 1959. 12.5 x 9.5 inches.

91

Wenn Sie wüßten, wie roh selbst gebildete
Menschen sich gegen die schätzbarsten Kunst-
werke verhalten, Sie würden mir verzeihen,
wenn ich die meinigen nicht unter die Menge
bringen mag. Niemand weiß eine Medaille
am Rand anzufassen; sie betasten das schön-
ste Gepräge, den reinsten Grund, lassen die
köstlichsten Stücke zwischen dem Daumen
und Zeigefinger hin- und hergehen, als wenn
man Kunstformen auf diese Weise prüfte.
Ohne daran zu denken, daß man ein großes
Blatt mit zwei Händen anfassen müsse,
greifen sie mit einer Hand nach einem un-
schätzbaren Kupferstich, einer unersetzlichen
Zeichnung. - Niemand denkt daran, daß wenn
nur zwanzig Menschen mit einem Kunst-
werke hintereinander ebenso verführen, der
einundzwanzigste nicht mehr viel daran zu
sehen hätte.

GOETHE

88

→ 88 Calligraphic broadside.
Text by Johann Wolfgang von Goethe. Written in the
style of Diotima Italic. The flourished majuscule letterforms were the basis for the Ariadne Initials typeface,
cut in metal by August Rosenberger. Not dated.
19 x 15.5 inches.

89 Diotima Italic type specimen.
Diotima Italic specimen showing the capital and lowercase alphabets, old-style figures and a sample setting
of the type. Released by D. Stempel AG in 1952.
11.75 x 8.25 inches.

90 Certificate for an award.
Printed certificate for the Friedenspreis des Deutschen
Buchhandels, designed using Diotima Italic for the body
text. The name of the recipient, Hermann Hesse, is set in
Smaragd and printed in color. 1955. 12.5 x 9.5 inches.

→ 91 Calligraphic design for exhibition poster.
Calligraphic design written in the style of Ariadne Initials
and Diotima Italic, used on a poster for an exhibition
of Gudrun Zapf von Hesse's work, held in 1998, in the
Hessische Landes- und Hochschulbibliothek, Darmstadt-
Schloss, Darmstadt, Germany. Not dated. 7.5 x 6.5 inches.

PFALZ KUNST
Dom Elch Halm
Guß West Bild
Vers Chintz Yak
JŒX ROM IQÆ

NOFRET ... ...   Mai 1985

93

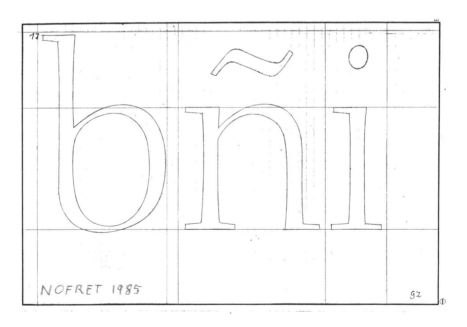

NOFRET 1985   92

94

Als Gußmarken
bezeichnet man kleine
Markierungen, die
sich gelegentlich an
der Seitenwand von
Erzeugnissen älterer
Schriftgießereien
befinden. Sie kamen
im letzten Drittel

des 19. Jahrhunderts auf und waren signifikant für den
Handmaschinenguß. Bei diesem Herstellungs–
verfahren verursacht ein flacher Stift in der Gießform
eine entsprechende stumpfe Vertiefung an der
Drucktype. Zwei Formen dieser Gußmarkierungen
haben sich herausgebildet: Zum einen wurden die
herstellungsbedingten Vertiefungen als »einfache«
Gußzeichen belassen, das heißt als runde, blinde
Felder an der Außenseite der Drucktypen. Zum
anderen wurden in einer weiteren Entwicklungsstufe
diese vertieften Blindfelder individuell gestaltet.
Die Gußmarke erschien so als Markenzeichen
mit Namenszug beziehungsweise Kurzangabe
der Herstellerfirma. Technische Innovationen
nach Einführung der Komplettgießmaschinen ließen
einige dieser Markierungen wieder verschwinden.
Nach der Jahrhundertwende blieben noch fünf der
alten Schriftgießereien bei der Gewohnheit,
Gußmarkierungen anzubringen, in einem Fall sogar
bis kurz nach dem Zweiten Weltkrieg.

98

NOFRET

92 Calligraphic broadside.
Text by Rochus Spiecker. The calligraphic forms in this
piece were the basis for the Nofret typeface. Not dated.
9.5 x 6.25.

→ 93 Drawing for Nofret Roman.
Capitals, lowercase and special characters arranged to
demonstrate letter and word spacing. Executed as a
proposal for the management of H. Berthold AG, Berlin,
Germany, who issued the typeface. May 1985.
8.25 x 11.75 inches.

→ 94 Drawing for Nofret Roman.
The lowercase letters b, n with tilde (diacritical mark for
Spanish language) and i, drawn in outline form in large
scale size for the Ikarus system used by H. Berthold AG.
Nofret was designed as a typeface for photocomposition
on H. Berthold AG equipment. 1985. 8.25 x 11.75 inches.

95 Drawing for Nofret Roman.
The letters O and N drawn in outline form in large-scale
size for the Ikarus system used by H. Berthold AG. 1985.
8.25 x 11.75.

96 Cover of type specimen book for Nofret.
The cover lists the different weights of the Nofret Roman,
Italic and small cap alphabets in which the type was
produced. *Nofret; Berthold Types, Probe 150.* H. Berthold AG,
Berlin, Germany, 1986. 11.75 x 8.25 inches.

97 Film for photocomposition typesetting.
Images of Nofret Mager (Light) appear on the film. This
is the finished film based type product used in photocomposition, manufactured by H. Berthold AG, Berlin.
Not dated. 3.75 x 2.25 inches.

→ 98 Page from *Der Polygraph.*
Special section of *Der Polygraph,* a trade journal for the
printing industry, published in Frankfurt am Main.
The topic is *Gussmarken,* the identifying casting marks
used by type foundries. Set in Nofret. Not dated.
11.75 x 8.25 inches.

100

99 Fachhochschule Hamburg brochure.
    Nofret was selected by the Fachhochschule in Hamburg,
    Germany, for use as the standard type for all its
    publications, including announcements, stationery and
    posters. Displayed is the cover of a promotional brochure
    for the Office for Research and Innovation, set in Nofret
    Roman and Italic. April 1998. 11 x 8.25 inches.

→ 100 Broadside with drawn lettering.
    Original lettering, drawn in pencil. The German phrase
    Frieden und Freiheit (Peace and Freedom). The word for
    peace is repeated in Latin, French, English and Spanish.
    This lettering was the first proposal for the bold version
    of Nofret Roman. Not dated. 15.75 x 19.75 inches.

A QUICK BROWN FOX JUMPS OVER THE LAZY DOG

a quick brown fox jumps over the lazy dog

a quick brown fox jumps over the lazy dog

101

105

bibliotheca christiana

106

1

A quick brown fox jumps over the lazy dog.

-1989

Gudrun Zapf von Hesse

107

ALCUIN

→ 105 Calligraphic broadside with cut-out letters.
Composition using the letterforms of Alcuin Roman.
Cut-out pen written letters mounted on paper leaf, on
which a large flourish was previously written. Quotation
by Horace, "Hora fugit, carpe diem" (Time flies, seize
the day). 1989. 17 x 12.5 inches, matted.

→ 106 Reproduction of publisher's device.
Prior to the development of the Alcuin Roman typeface,
Gudrun Zapf employed the same style in hand lettering
the design of "bibliotheca christiana," a device for Verlag
Bibliotheca Christiana, Bonn, Germany. Not dated.
4.25 x 10 inches.

→ 107 Drawing of lowercase letters for Alcuin Roman.
An alphabet sentence showing all the lowercase letters
for Alcuin Roman and to test spacing, for URW Typeface
and Software GmbH, Hamburg, Germany. 1989.
11.5 x 8 inches.

108 Drawing of capital letters for Alcuin Roman.
Large-scale letters Ä, Y and J, drawn in outline to the
size required for digitization by URW using the Ikarus
System. Ikarus is a program for typeface design
developed by Dr. Peter Karow. 1990. 8.25 x 11.75 inches.

109 Drawing of lowercase letters for Alcuin Roman.
Large-scale letters ö, ü and g, drawn in outline to the
size required for digitization by URW using the Ikarus
System. 1990. 8.25 x 11.75 inches.

→ 110 Advertisement for Alcuin Roman.
First URW advertisement for the typeface, with a history of Carolingian minuscule letters and a description of the making of Alcuin Roman. Not dated. 16.5 x 11.5 inches.

→ 111 Print with proof letters for Alcuin Roman.
Quotation by Wassily Kandinsky. The proof letters show a version of Alcuin Roman with thinner hairline strokes than those used for the finished typeface. Not dated. 3.75 x 8 inches.

Buchstaben sind praktische
und nützliche Zeichen,
aber ebenso reine Form
und innere Melodie.

WASSILY KANDINSKY

111

Viel Glück zum neuen Jahre.

Lassen Sie uns dieses zubringen, wie wir das vorige

beendet haben, mit wechselseitiger Teilnahme

an dem, was wir lieben und treiben.

Der neue Kalender steht vor mir, wo die zwölf Monate zwar reinlich

aber auch vollkommen gleichgültig aussehen. Vergebens forsch ich,

welche Tage sich für mich rot, welche düster sich färben werden;

die ganze Tafel ist noch in Blanco, indessen Wünsche und Hoffnungen

hin und wieder schwärmen. Möge sich dem Erfüllen und Gelingen

nichts! nichts! entgegen setzen!

Es gibt kein Vergangenes, das man zurücksehnen

dürfte, es gibt nur ein ewig Neues,

das sich aus den erweiterten Elementen

Johann Wolfgang von Goethe   des Vergangenen gestaltet.

Mit allen guten Wünschen für das Jahr 1995 von Gudrun und Hermann Zapf

112

Wilder Rosenbusch

Wie steht er da vor den Verdunkelungen
des Regenabends, jung und rein;
in seinen Ranken schenkend ausgeschwungen
und doch versunken in sein Rose-sein;

die flachen Blüten, da und dort schon offen,
jegliche ungewollt und ungepflegt:
so, von sich selbst unendlich übertroffen
und unbeschreiblich aus sich selbst erregt,

ruft er dem Wandrer, der in abendlicher
Nachdenklichkeit den Weg vorüberkommt:
Oh sieh mich stehn, sieh her, was bin ich sicher
und unbeschützt und habe was mir frommt.

Rainer Maria Rilke

116

COLOMBINE

→ 116 Calligraphic broadside.
Informal calligraphy or handwriting of "Wilder
Rosenbusch" by Rainer Maria Rilke. The design of the
Colombine typeface is based on Gudrun Zapf von Hesse's
handwriting. Not dated. 12.25 x 9.25.

Mode Athen Sage Clavigo Haus
Requiem Byzanz Quadrat Abt !
Zopf Pax Null Darmstadt X?
Wespe Uhu Xylo Liqueur Spaß O
DTV FILZ Quote KYOGA Joga
183459067 £ $ V YFQ Eq irpe g
£ & & 128974206 Zweck ck c jn
123

117

→ 117 Study for Colombine.
       Reproduction of handwritten letterforms, enlarged
       and mounted to compare combinations of letters and
       numbers. Not dated. 8.25 x 11.75.

  118 Calligraphic broadside.
       Freely written experimental calligraphy, produced while
       the Colombine typeface was in development. Not dated.
       13.75 x 11 inches, matted.

  119 Drawing for proposed bold version of Colombine.
       Sample letters drawn to test hairline weights and letter
       spacing for a proposed bold version of Colombine.
       1989. 8.25 x 11.75.

4

MODETZK
JOGAFYRE
DILQUVPC

Hermann Zapf von Hesse 1989

120

→ 120 Drawing of capitals for Colombine.
Drawing for Colombine in the regular weight. An
alternative character for the letter O appears on the sheet.
1989. 8.25 x 11.75 inches.

121 Drawing of figures for Colombine.
Drawing for Colombine figures in the regular weight;
alternatives for various figures are shown in the drawing.
1989. 8.25 x 11.75 inches.

122 Drawing of upper and lowercase characters
for Colombine.
Drawing for Colombine in the regular weight; alternative
characters are included in the drawing, as well as letter
combinations to test spacing. 1989. 8.25 x 11.75 inches.

123 Drawing of capitals for Colombine Light.
The letters G and M drawn in outline form to large-scale
size for digitization on the Ikarus system. Not dated.
8.25 x 11.75 inches.

124 Drawing of lowercase letters for Colombine.
The letters m, g, and i, with their connecting strokes.
Drawn in outline form to large-scale size for digitization
on the Ikarus system. Not dated. 8.25 x 11.75 inches.

125 Drawing of capital letters for Colombine Bold.
The character Œ (a ligature of the diphthong o and e) and
F drawn in outline form in large-scale size for digitization
on the Ikarus system. Not dated. 8.25 x 11.75 inches.

126 Drawing of figures for Colombine Bold.
The figures 6, 2 and 8, drawn to size for digitization on
the Ikarus system. Not dated. 8.25 x 11.75 inches.

127 Computer print of Colombine Light.
Settings of the typeface displayed in four different sizes,
9, 12, 18 and 24 point. This specimen sheet is a prelimi-
nary proof, without the kerning of letters. Not dated.
10.5 x 8.25 inches.

Too many types in use today betray the fact
that their designers were not conversant
with the early forms of letters,
that they had a feeble invention,
a weak sense of proportion or propriety.
Eccentricity of form from the hand of an artist
who is master of himself
and of his subject may be pleasing;
it becomes only mere affectation
when attempted by the ignorant amateur.

128

Too many types in use today betray the fact
that their designers were not conversant
with the early forms of letters,
that they had a feeble invention,
a weak sense of proportion or propriety.
Eccentricity of form from the hand of an artist
who is master of himself
and of his subject may be pleasing;
it becomes only mere affectation
when attempted by the ignorant amateur.

129

→ 128   Type specimen of Colombine Light.
Designed to show the characteristic connecting strokes
of the typeface. Quotation by Frederic W. Goudy. 1991.
11.75 x 8.25 inches.

→ 129   Type specimen of Colombine Bold.
Designed to show the characteristic connecting strokes
of the typeface. Quotation by Frederic W. Goudy. 1991.
11.75 x 8.25 inches.

130

Galahad Regular

ABCDEFGHIJKL
MNOPQRSTUV
WXYZabcdefghijk
lmnopqrstuvwxyz
&1234567890

Galahad Oldstyle Figures
(the characters that differ from the Regular set)

1234567890$¢£¥f
#%‰

Galahad Alternate (The small letters below each character indicate the keyboard access position. ◊ indicates shift position.)

Below: The full character set for Galahad Regular. Galahad Oldstyle Figures contains a full character set, with old style figures and accompanying monetary signs replacing those in the Regular character set. Galahad Alternate contains variations on many of the uppercase and lowercase letters and several useful ligatures.

ABCDEFGHIJKLM
NOPQRSTUVWX
YZabcdefghijklmno
pqrstuvwxyz&1234
567890ÆŒØæœø
fiflßₐᵃ°$¢£¥f¤/%‰
#°.^~<±>=+¬.,;:!?¿¡
,„——‹‹›»()[]{}|\
_…†‡§¶*•@©®™´ˆˋ˜¨
˘˙˝¸ÁÂÄÀÅÃÇÉÊ
ËÈÍÎÏÑÓÔÖÒÚ
ÛÜÙŸáâäàåãçéêè
íîïñóôöòõúûüùÿ

GALAHAD

Alan Blackman

Alan Blackman began his study of letterforms as a student at the California College of Arts and Crafts in Oakland, California in the late 1950s, where he excelled at brush lettering. He found many opportunities to exercise this craft, working at the Phoebe A. Hearst Anthropology Museum at the University of California at Berkeley, and at Flax Art Supply Store in San Francisco. He has been active in the Friends of Calligraphy since the 1970s, and has served in many of its executive positions. The Friends conferred the status of Honorary Membership on him in 1995.

He taught for many years at the San Francisco Academy of Art College, and now travels widely, teaching lettering and design workshops in North America, Europe, and Japan. The titles of his classes reveal his evangelism for the magic of making letters: "Roman Caps Without Tears," "How Far Is Far Out?" and "Calligraphic Tapestries." Blackman's lettering clients include brokerage firms, churches, restaurants, and greeting card companies. Examples of his calligraphic artwork are found in the Harrison Collection of Calligraphy of the San Francisco Public Library, the library of the Victoria and Albert Museum in London, and in private collections.

In 1967, as a way of enlivening his correspondence with his young son Stephen, Blackman began designing one of a kind, hand decorated envelopes for philatelic first day covers. To preserve his ideas, he also made duplicate envelopes addressed to himself. These have grown into a large collection of whimsical and fantastic creations reflecting the design of the newly issued postage stamps. The collection has been exhibited at several international calligraphy conferences, and examples have been published in *Letter Arts Review* and *Upper & Lower Case.*

Blackman designed his typeface Galahad for Adobe Systems in 1995. The staff at Adobe invited him to design the face after viewing his envelope collection. Though Blackman's lettering on the envelopes often includes violin-playing As and baseball-pitching Bs, the staff at Adobe saw potential in the neatly lettered, rough-edged, relatively straightforward Roman caps and lowercase. Blackman credits Hermann Zapf's Optima typeface and Friedrich Neugebauer's flat-pen Roman calligraphy as having influenced this style. In addition to lettering with the pen and brush, Blackman's interests include opera, German literature, and twentieth century painting and cinema.

I saw Hermann Zapf's work for the first time in 1960 when I was a student of brush lettering at the California College of Arts and Crafts. Our instructor had told us of the Zapf exhibition in the former San Francisco Museum of Modern Art, on the top floor of the War Memorial Building in the Civic Center. The sketches for the typeface Optima impressed me profoundly. Zapf set before me a standard of beauty and elegance to which I have aspired ever since. A.B.

The knights knelt, filled with an
overwhelming sense of peace and tranquillity.
Then a mighty voice rang out:
"DRAW NEAR THE GRAIL, SIR GALAHAD,
regular with alternates 27.27

Adobe Systems introduces a new
typeface in the Adobe Originals library

GALAHAD

for all your life has been a preparation for
this moment. You are without pride, greed,
cowardice and all the weaknesses of men.
regular 17.14

Drink from the cup, Sir Galahad,
regular 39 pt.

earthly guardian of this most sacred relic.
Guard it well, so that only worthy men may
look upon it in its full glory. For in it they will
glimpse the PARADISE which all men seek."
regular with alternates 21.25

131

→ 131 Galahad type specimen booklet.
Illustrated here are two panels from the reverse side of
the specimen booklet. This side of booklet is designed as
a poster, with sample settings of Galahad in sizes from
14 point to 160 point. Text extracts from *Knights,* by Julek
Heller and Dierdre Headon. 1995. 9 x 34 inches.

132 Drawing for Galahad.
Original unretouched calligraphy. Developmental
lettering for Galahad written with green stick ink. 1992.
12.5 x 8.5 inches.

133 Proof sheet for Galahad.
Includes notes by Adobe design staff for corrections to
individual characters. Digitization of Galahad was
done by Linnea Lundquist and Kathleen Foster, with art
direction from Alan Blackman and Carol Twombly.
1994. 11 x 8.5 inches.

134 Photograph of restaurant sign.
Kites restaurant, near Civic Center, San Francisco,
showing use of Galahad for its signage. 2000. 4 x 7 inches.

135 Beasts of Paradise, *Gathered on the Edge.*
Galahad used for compact disk booklet title and text,
also for title on the disk. Published by City of Tribes,
San Francisco. 1995. 5 x 5.5 inches.

136 Title for *The Buddha Box.*
Galahad used for title on box containing book and
small statue. It is also used for the book title and chapter
headings. *The Buddha Box.* Manuela Dunn Mascetti. San
Francisco, Chronicle Books, 1998. 6.75 x 4 x 2.75 inches.

137 Title for *Batman & Demon: A Tragedy.*
Galahad used for the title on a comic book cover,
published by DC Comics, New York, 2000.
10.25 x 6.75 inches.

138

140

→138 First day cover for Richard Nixon commemorative stamp.
Original calligraphy, written with stick ink and watercolor. For each envelope Alan Blackman created a unique
calligraphic design to reflect the subject of the stamp.
These examples of Blackman's calligraphy led Adobe to
commission Galahad. 1995. 4 x 7.5 inches.

139 First day cover for 32 cent Love stamp.
Original calligraphy, written with stick ink and watercolor.
1995. 4 x 7.5 inches.

→140 First day cover for Louis Armstrong
commemorative stamp.
Original calligraphy, written with stick ink and watercolor. 1995. 4 x 7.5 inches.

141 First day cover for *Legends of American Music: Songwriters*
commemorative stamps.
Original calligraphy, written with stick ink and watercolor. 1996. 4 x 7.5 inches.

142

KOSMIK

→ 142 Kosmik type specimen.
The typeface has regular and bold weights with three variations for each, a font with Flipper software in each weight and a set of ornaments. Kosmik was released by FontShop International in 1993. Type specimen designed by John D. Berry. 2001. 16.5 x 11.5 inches.

Erik van Blokland

Erik van Blokland, a Dutch type designer, studied Graphic and Typographic Design at the Royal Academy for Fine and Applied Arts in The Hague. He was encouraged to pursue type design by his teacher Gerrit Noordzij, who is well known for his scholarship on calligraphic origins and his theories about the influence of the hand in the making of letterforms. In the early 1990s, Van Blokland started the design company LettError with his friend and fellow Noordzij student, Just van Rossum. They experimented together to develop a randomizing computer program that they used in the design of the type family Beowolf. This typeface created a stir in the typographic world because the individual characters change shape randomly every time they are printed.

Van Blokland has published many typefaces with FontShop International, including Beowolf, Kosmik, Erikrighthand, Trixie, and Zapata. The typeface Trixie, based on the shapes made by a manual typewriter, rose to cult status when used for the X in the title logo for the television series X-Files. Erikrighthand, based on Van Blokland's own rough handwriting, was one of the first typefaces of this style to become internationally popular. With Just van Rossum and Petr van Blokland, Erik is a key developer of the font editing software Robofog. The partners use their programming skills to implement their design concepts.

Projects by LettError include development of a calendar machine for KPN Dutch Telecom, a visual noise machine for MTV Europe, and a layout-grid fitter for the 1999 Dutch Christmas stamps. LettError also produces the TypoMan and Crocodile show, about a typographic superhero and his cold-blooded sidekick who protect the world against big words, flying arrows and hopping lamps. The show is recorded in front of a live audience and is produced in PoppeKast, another technology developed by LettError. Erik van Blokland and his partners have found innovative ways to get computers and type to do the exciting, random, and fun things that the human hand does.

I studied type design with Gerrit Noordzij. Noordzij sees type design as a logical progression from writing, so the classes started with calligraphy, broad nib brushes, and pens. I learned to appreciate the human quality of the hand and, together with Just van Rossum, developed ways to keep the imperfection, variation and liveliness in digital fonts. Mechanical methods of producing typography made calligraphy different from type design. However, electronic type offers us a way to combine a love of handmade type with modern digital tools. One such system, Flipper, is a program embedded in the font which switches between alternatives for each letter, to ensure that no identical shapes end up next to or near each other. The typeface FF Kosmik was specially designed to work with this technology – three hand-drawn sans serif typefaces that work as one. Kosmik does not automate calligraphy but brings some of the attractions of handmade type to typography. E.V.B.

ABCDEFGHIJKLMNOPQRSTUVWXYZ\^∨~
abcdefghijklmno pqrst uvwxyz

, ¢§ß ÆŒæœ→ ~fi{}[]£fl &

¶¤%ªºTM¥‹›"ºƒ!"#$+‼ ()†‒*❀…
,·/0123456789 :;=?☆ ⚡▦@®©℗

143

→ 143 Drawing for Kosmik.
Original lettering for a single weight of Kosmik. Pen
drawing on tracing vellum. 1993. 11.75 x 16.5 inches.

144 Kosmik type specimen booklet.
Cover of booklet, subtitled "it moves, it animates, it's
a typeface, it is a FontFont." Published by LettError and
FontShop International. 1992. 5.5 x 3.75 inches.

→ 145 Page opening of Kosmik type specimen booklet.
Demonstration of Kosmik characters and symbols
combined for graphic design applications. 1992.
5.5 x 3.75 inches.

→ 146 Page opening from *The LettError Book.*
Typographic composition using Kosmik. Text on facing
page describes Flipper software. LettError won the
2000 Charles Nypels Award. Part of the prize was the
publication of this book about their work by Drukkerij
Rosbeek, Nuth, Netherlands. 2000. 7.75 x 7.75 inches.

147 Book jacket for *How To Say No Without Feeling Guilty.*
Book jacket designed using Kosmik. Title of book and
text on jacket and flaps set in Kosmik. The jacket was
designed by Matteo Bologna. *How To Say No Without
Feeling Guilty.* Patti Breitman and Connie Hatch.
Broadway Books, New York, 2000. 8.5 x 20.5 inches.

148 T-shirt logo.
Kosmik used on T-shirt made for Virtual Valley, a San
Jose electronic bulletin board company. Not dated. Extra
large size; old, worn by the designer, but clean.

149 Classroom lettering demonstration.
Original lettering. Teaching exercise, done at the Graphic
and Typographic Design Department, Royal Academy
for Fine and Applied Arts, The Hague. Written with
black marking pen and highlighted in red. Not dated.
8.25 x 11.75 inches.

From the FF Kosmik specimen ©LettError

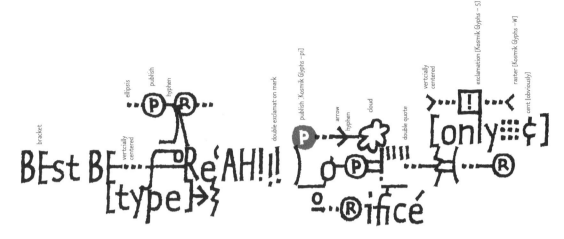

Some of the special symbols in Kosmik are shown on this page. Look around in the fonts for other characters.

Make **modern** hieroglyphs by combining different elements of the typeface. Several characters can be put together to create new symbols and shapes.

TRY KOSMIK
→ add text to illustrations
→ dialog in comics
→ comments in plans & maps
→ animated text

The book went that way ⮕

145

Hee!! daar gaat een Onomatopee! He mmderdemmderdemm! en stiekem a an zeeëgels denken en eidereendeiere n zoeken, of aan sauerstoffflaschen snuffelen en de Schifffahrt nog een bekijken. TOEOEOET! Verdraaid, net t e laat. TAATUU!! AAARGH!? ❧⋯→ IIIEEE!! KLABAM!? Flippperende jazzzangeres Anna wauwelt tegen Otto. Pffff! Daa r gaat hij! Krokodil, snel er achter aa n! WOEF! Ho stop mannetje! Jij bent e rbij! "Verdrie" VRRROOOAAARRR! Ze zi tten vlak achter ons! Harder, harder! Een bom! Zo! Daar heeft hij aldus de j

146

150

NYX

→ 150 Nyx type specimen.
Nyx, named for the Greek goddess of night, is based
on stencil letterforms. Released by Adobe Systems in
1997. Type specimen designed by Rick Cusick. 2001.
18 x 12 inches.

Rick Cusick

Rick Cusick began his lettering career designing illuminated signs in his hometown of Stockton, California, followed by study at Art Center College of Design in Los Angeles. Since 1971 he has worked in lettering and typographic design and as a book designer for Hallmark Cards, Inc., in Kansas City, Missouri. As the lettering studio manager, his duties include overseeing font development. He has designed several proprietary typefaces for Hallmark that are used on a range of products such as greeting cards, books, films, and packaging. From 1984 to 1990 he taught typography and publication design at the University of Kansas.

Cusick has also compiled, edited, and designed two books about prominent twentieth century American calligraphers: *With Respect…To RFD,* an appreciation of Raymond F. DaBoll; and *Straight Impressions,* essays and calligraphy by Lloyd Reynolds. Another book, *The Proverbial Bestiary,* features proverbs hand lettered by Cusick, paired with drawings by the late Warren Chappell. He has been the art director of *Letter Arts Review* since 1992, and has brought that journal to a level of excellence in its layout and design that honors the integrity of its calligraphic, typographic, and editorial content. Cusick's own calligraphic style is immediately recognizable for its verve and confidence.

Nyx is a stencil typeface named after Cusick's muse, the Greek goddess of night. Like others in the design professions, Cusick works constantly, often late into the night, and his type design projects evolve in nocturnal hours when interruptions are unwelcome from anyone but his muse. The stencil characters were originally drawn using Adobe Illustrator software. He tested the shapes frequently in his graphic design projects of the early 1990s, looking for the best variations in widths, weights, and character shapes. Adobe Systems released the typeface in 1997.

Calligraphy confirms a certain inevitability to the construction of letterforms – as important in the west as the chromatic scale and just as rich in its potential for personal expression. For me, it is a touchstone by which to compare and contrast all explorations, whether for personal use or the development of a new font. Sometimes, as in the case of Nyx, it turns out to be for both. R.C.

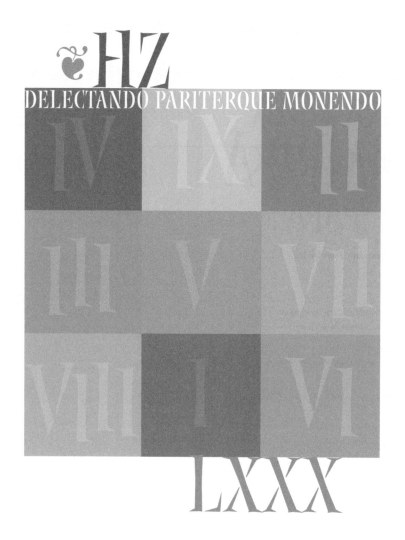

152

151 Untitled.
     Collage of computer prints. First digital version of the
     letterforms, which developed into Nyx. Latin quotation
     with translation, "The times change and we change with
     them." A tribute to Hermann Zapf, for "Lettering Arts
     in the Zapf Tradition," an exhibition sponsored by the
     Washington Calligraphers Guild, Washington, D.C.
     1993. 11 x 16 inches.

→ 152 Page from *The Magic Constant.*
       Typographic composition with magic square, roman
       numerals. Part of a series of nine prints designed using
       Nyx. Quotation by Horace: *delectando pariterque monendo*
       (by giving pleasure and at the same time instruction).
       From *The Magic Constant, A Birthday Suite of Magic Squares
       for Hermann Zapf.* Rick Cusick. Nyx Editions, Kansas City,
       Missouri, 1998. 11.75 by 8.5 inches.

QUIET PASSION:
A Twenty-Five Year Retrospective
of the Work of RICK CUSICK,
Calligrapher & Graphic Designer

August 1st through September 30, 1995

The San Francisco Public Library,
Civic Center · Third Floor

NA VIDYA*
MATRIKA
PARA

Library Hours:
  Sunday: 12-5
  Monday: 10-6
  Tuesday · Wednesday · Thursday: 9-8
  Friday: 11-5
  Saturday: 9-5

Co-sponsored by The Special Collections Department &
The Friends of the San Francisco Public Library

"There is no knowledge beyond the alphabet."   *(from the Sanskrit)*

153

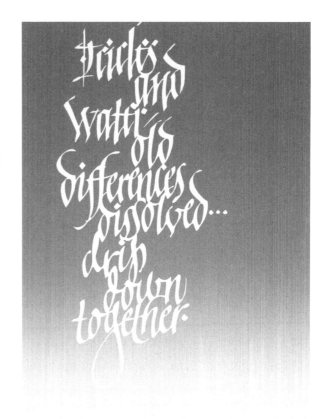

156

→ 153 Exhibition announcement for *Quiet Passion: A Twenty-five Year Retrospective of the Work of Rick Cusick*.
Printed card for an exhibition at the San Francisco Public Library. Calligraphy, lettering and design by Rick Cusick. The stencil letterforms drawn for the Sanskrit quotation are the basis of the typeface Nyx. The text typeface is Adobe Caslon. 1995. 6 x 4 inches.

154 Title for *Ghosts Adrift*.
Titling and title page designed using Nyx. *Ghosts Adrift*. Thaddeus Strode. Kunstverein Heilbronn, Oktagon Verlag, Cologne, Germany, 2000. 7.75 x 6 inches.

155 Page from *The Magic Constant*.
Typographic composition with magic square, Arabic numbers. Part of a series of nine prints designed using Nyx. From *The Magic Constant, A Birthday Suite of Magic Squares for Hermann Zapf*. Rick Cusick. Nyx Editions, Kansas City, Missouri, 1998. 11.75 by 8.5 inches.

→ 156 *Spring*.
Calligraphic silkscreen print. Haiku by Teishitsu. 1989. 22.25 x 14.5 inches.

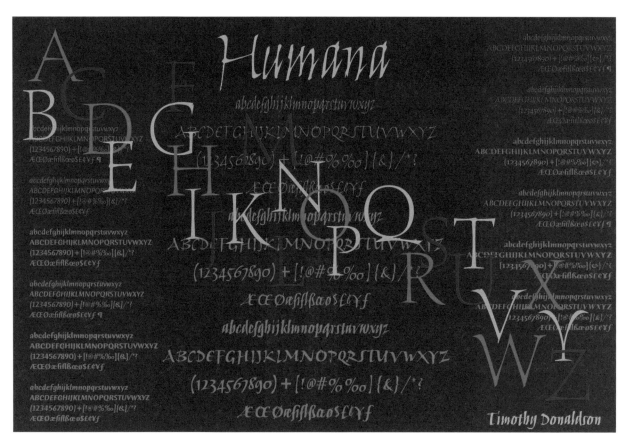

157

HUMANA

→ 157 Humana type specimen.
Specimen shows the type families of Humana Serif,
Humana Sans and Humana Script. Colored Humana
Serif capitals on a dark background. Humana was
released by ITC in 1995. Type specimen designed by
Kathleen Burch. 2001. 12 x 18 inches.

Timothy Donaldson

Timothy Donaldson is a self-taught lettering artist who has been writing for more than twenty years. His first lettering career was as a sign painter, but his desire to experiment with more detailed lettering propelled him into a second career as a type designer (he also credits Hermann Zapf for encouragement to pursue that direction).

His calligraphic type designs include Banshee and Immi 505 for Adobe Systems, FancyWriting for FontShop International, Cyberkugel, Digital Woodcuts, Humana, and Riptide for ITC, and Etruscan, Flight, John Handy, Klee, Ru'ach, and Ulysses for Esselte Corporation.

Over the years his creative and professional endeavors have expanded and he has taken on teaching, graphic design, sculpture, painting, and making digital paintings with Photoshop software on the computer. His inspirations for artwork involving letterforms come from contemporary German and Eastern European calligraphers. He teaches graphic design, handwriting, lettering, and type design at Stafford College in England. Examples of his calligraphy and typographic works have been published in *Letter Arts Review, Print, I.D., Upper & Lower Case, Creative Review,* and *Eye.* At the conference for the Association Typographique Internationale in Reading, England in 1997, he created what he called "the world's biggest hamburgefonts," a huge sampling of his spiky handwriting, written with a two-foot handmade brush on a triple roll of butcher paper. Donaldson has won awards for his type designs from the Morisawa International Type Design Competitions in 1996 and 1999, and from the Type Directors Club in 1997.

Humana is an extended family with fifteen weights and styles (light, medium, and bold weights of a serif, sans serif and script design, with matching italics for the serif and sans serif). Donaldson initially created the Humana Script typeface with a broad-edged pen, and then drew corresponding roman and sans serif versions as pencil sketches prior to constructing and refining the characters on a computer screen.

Calligraphy is to type as illustration is to clip art: Yes, my friends, type is clip art. This began to sink in when I first printed a letter in one of my handwriting typefaces. I was quite shocked at the repetitive rigidity and sterility of the page. Years earlier, when I started to do calligraphy, I was keen to get every letter looking the same. This continued until the clip art epiphany and a remark made by one of my students concerning a large italic model I'd written in class: "It looks just like it was printed." Ah ha! Since then I have tried to make sure that every letter is different. One day, market forces permitting, I might be able to do a similar thing with type. T.D.

158

→ 158 Humana type specimen.
Specimen shows the type families of Humana Serif, Humana Sans and Humana Script. Colored Humana Script capitals on a light background. Type specimen designed by Kathleen Burch. 2001. 8 x 12 inches.

159 Page opening from *The Little Network Book for Windows and Macintosh.*
Text of book set in Humana Sans Medium; margin notations set in Humana Italic and Bold. Illustration by John Grimes. *The Little Network Book for Windows and Macintosh.* Lon Poole and John Rizzo, Peachpit Press, Berkeley, California, 1999. 9.25 x 7.5 inches.

→ 160 *Bloodbrotherhood.*
Calligraphic broadside. Calligraphic artwork drawn with computer software with line of text set in Humana Serif Light. Text paraphrases a quotation by Hermann Zapf, "…there is always a little drop of heart blood in the ink we use." 2001. 11.75 x 12.5 inches.

→ 161 *Karma Police.*
Calligraphic broadside. Original calligraphy, written with black ink on fluorescent-colored paper. Includes wax seal. 2001. 20 x 25 inches.

WITH A LITTLE DROP OF HEARTBLOOD IN OUR INK

160

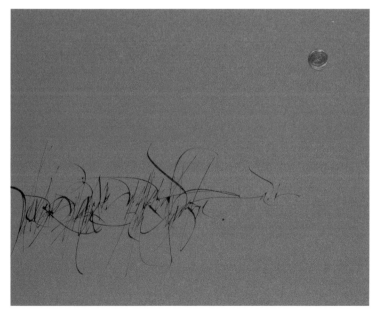

161

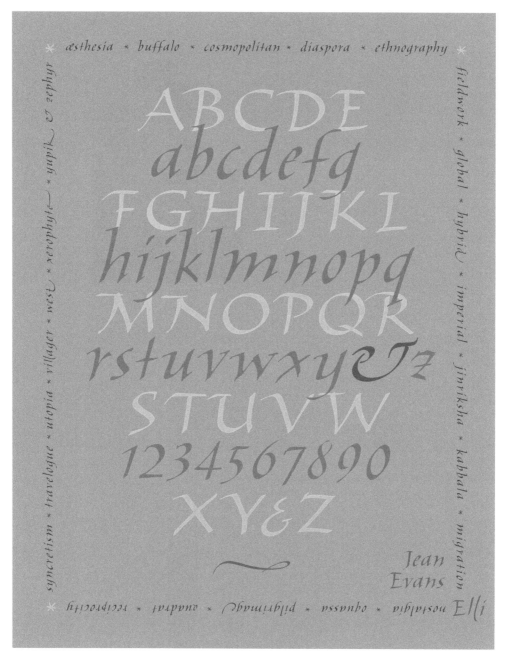

162

ELLI

→ 162 Elli type specimen.
Single weight typeface based on the italic calligraphy
of Jean Evans. Originally commissioned in 1989 by
the Houghton Library, Harvard University, in honor
of Eleanor Garvey, Curator Emerita, of the library's
Department of Printing and Graphic Arts. Released
for general use by Font Bureau in 1993. Type specimen
designed by Kathleen Burch. 2001. 14 x 11 inches.

Jean Evans

Jean Evans, originally from South Carolina, studied art history at Queens College in Charlotte, North Carolina. She then moved to Cambridge, Massachusetts and, after a season playing the European tennis circuit, became the tennis coach at Radcliffe College. She was a nationally ranked tennis player in the 1960s and 1970s.

Evans has worked in type design and production at Bitstream and Interleaf. Her type designs include Elli, Dizzy and Rats (released by Font Bureau), and Hatmaker (released by Agfa/Monotype). Elli was Evans's first original typeface, and is based on her personal italic hand. It was commissioned in 1989 by the Houghton Library at Harvard University to honor Eleanor Garvey at the time of her retirement as Curator of Printing & Graphic Arts. The face was completed in 1991, and was used exclusively by Eleanor Garvey and the Houghton Library until Font Bureau adapted it for commercial distribution in 1993. The typeface Dizzy grew out of an artist's book commission about the jazz trumpeter Dizzy Gillespie, a long-time friend from Evans's home state. She was attracted to Gillespie's gnarled, peculiar handwriting, and worked directly from samples of his handwriting to fill out the character set. Rats is also based on a particular individual's handwriting, that of colleague Scott Nash, who is an artist and children's book illustrator. The Hatmaker family is comprised of two all-capital fonts, one inspired by Ben Shahn's hand-constructed alphabet, and the other created by Evans to be a complementary face.

Evans says she chose a profession in letterforms because of a third grade fascination with "fancy script writing." Since the third grade she has come a long way in fine-tuning her robust, dancing, breezy calligraphic style. She studied with David Howells, Hermann Zapf and Matthew Carter, and her work has been exhibited and collected worldwide. She works today as a freelance type designer and book artist in Cambridge. In her spare time she works in her daughter's school inspiring kindergartners to the joys of fancy writing, and introducing middle schoolers to the personality of typographic forms.

Jean Evans with Eleanor Garvey.

As a designer and artist, I always wanted to pin down those dancing and invented letters I made by hand. Many had such fortuitous quirks that were difficult to recreate. Thus, the idea to design Elli came about in 1985, while I was working at Bitstream. The bouncing baseline, the dance-like quality of the letters, the little flicks and puddles of ink that all calligraphers are familiar with when they write, were particularly important elements for me to incorporate in Elli, my first attempt at the craft of type design. J.E.

Susan Bennett Book Fund

B O S T O N   A T H E N A E U M

164

163 Calligraphic invitation.
Printed card for an event at the Fogg Art Museum,
Harvard University. Designed using italic calligraphy.
1984. 4.5 x 6.5 inches.

→ 164 Calligraphic label for Susan Bennett Book Fund.
Printed label for the Boston Athenaeum. Designed using
italic calligraphy, with decorative calligraphic flourish.
1989. 2.25 x 4 inches.

Calligraphy into Type

Wednesday, 4 March 1992, at The Club of Odd Volumes

The Society of Printers presents a Talk by Jean Evans
about her typeface commissioned by the Departm

Please respond by Friday, 28 February to the Secretary, Eugene R. Bailey, at 508 655 6287.

Reservations not honored will be invoiced at the current fee.

166

165 Typographic invitation.
Printed card for an event held in the Houghton Library,
Harvard University. Designed using Elli. 1993.
4.75 x 6.25 inches.

→ 166 Announcement for Calligraphy Into Type.
Announcement for a talk by Jean Evans sponsored by
The Society of Printers, Boston. Letterpress printed card
set in Elli, with calligraphic background decoration by
Jean Evans. 1992. 5 x 20.75 inches.

Much madness
is divinest sense to a discerning eye—
much sense the starkest madness. Tis the majority
in this as all prevail. Assent and you are sane.
Demur, you're straightway dangerous
and handled with a chain. EMILY DICKINSON

169

167 Invitation for an author's book signing.
     Printed card designed using Elli, in combination with
     Charlemagne, a display type designed by Carol Twombly.
     1994. 6 x 9.25 inches.

168 Book jacket for *The Muse That Sings.*
     Elli typeface used for title and author's name. Jacket
     designed by Joy Taylor. *The Muse That Sings.* Ann
     McCutchan. New York, Oxford University Press, 1999.
     9.5 x 21 inches.

→ 169 Poem by Emily Dickinson.
     Original calligraphic broadside. Written with black ink
     and watercolor, with large brush-written initial. 1980.
     18 x 22 inches, framed.

ITC Kendo

designed by Phill Grimshaw

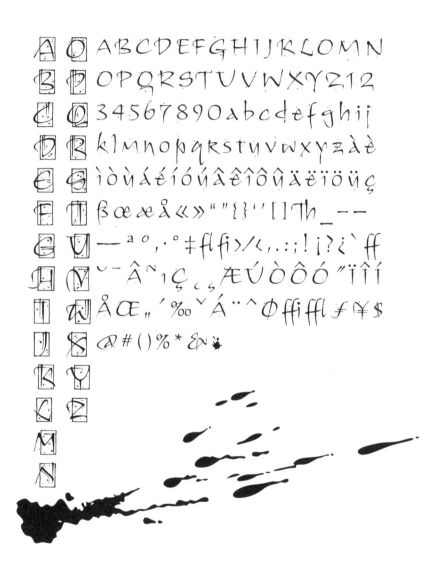

KENDO

→ 170 Kendo type specimen.
Single weight typeface with a set of initials. Released by
ITC in 1997. Type specimen designed by John D. Berry.
2001. 18 x 12 inches.

Phill Grimshaw

The late Phill Grimshaw studied at the Royal College
of Art in London, where he earned a Master of Arts
degree. He returned to his native Manchester, England
to work as a lettering artist and to develop a specializa-
tion in type design. His early designs include Oberon
and Hazel, released as dry-transfer lettering by Esselte
Corporation. When computer drawing programs for
type design became available, he used them, along
with pens and brushes, to design a total of forty-four
families for Esselte Corporation and ITC.

His designs strongly reflect his calligraphic training
as well as his imagination for dynamic letterforms.
Kendo was released by ITC in 1997. It suggests the
dash of quickly written calligraphy, made by a confident hand on rough paper, with ink spatters tossed in
random patterns. Despite its quickly written appearance, Grimshaw worked slowly and deliberately to
make the drawings, using a pen overloaded with ink,
applying pressure at the beginning of strokes and light-
ening his touch at the terminals. The nib frequently
caught on the rough surface of the paper; the resulting
splashes were then refined.

Grimshaw's other calligraphically inspired designs
for ITC include Braganza, Grimshaw Hand, Kallos,
Obelisk, Regallia, Samuel, and Tempus; and Arriba,
Gravura, Pristina, Scriptease, Zaragoza, and Zennor
for Esselte Corporation. In the mid 1990s, after con-
ducting research at the Glasgow School of Art, he produced a set of fonts based on the handwritten panels
from drawings and artwork of the Scottish architect,
Charles Rennie Mackintosh.

In addition to his work in lettering and type design,
Phill Grimshaw was also interested in the study of
the many megalithic monuments to be found in the
United Kingdom and Europe, ranging from mysteri-
ous and imposing structures such as Stonehenge, to
obscure stones located in other regions of the Northern
European countryside. He loved music, and played
the mandolin and guitar. He died in 1998 after a long
struggle with cancer. When his widow Penny was
asked to provide materials for this exhibition, she responded: "I know he particularly admired Hermann
Zapf. I'm really pleased that Phill is to be included
in this exhibition and he would be too."

*If you enjoy doing something and you're lucky enough
to be good at it, just do it for that reason.* P.G.

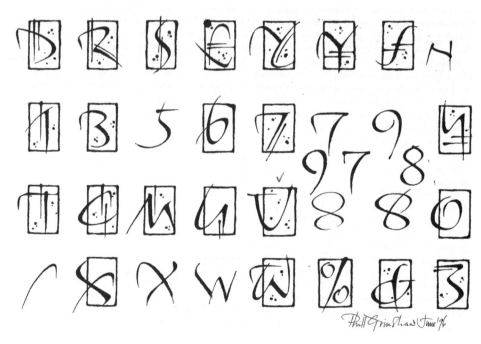

171

173

174

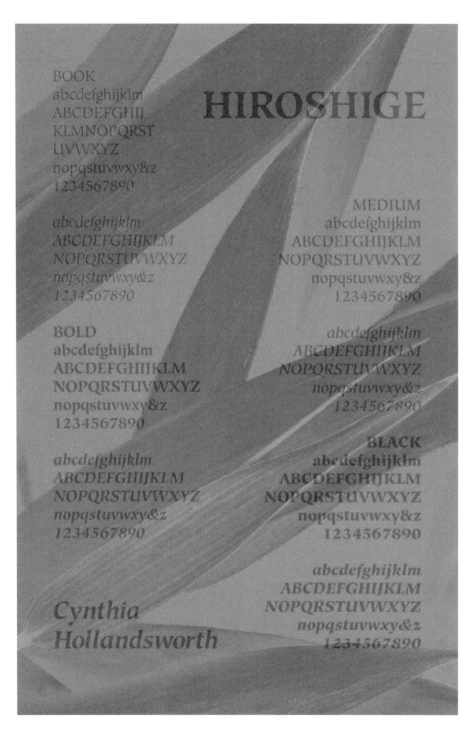

HIROSHIGE

→ 177 Hiroshige type specimen.
Hiroshige was originally released by AlphaOmega
Typography in 1986. Type specimen designed by
Kathleen Burch. 2001. 18 x 12 inches.

Cynthia Hollandsworth

Cynthia Hollandsworth was the editor of the magazine *Calligraphy Idea Exchange* (CIE) in the early 1980s (the magazine later became *Letter Arts Review*). As a calligrapher and associate of Arthur Baker, Hollandsworth was in a unique position to consider the value and validity of his theories on pen manipulation. She also wrote articles on this subject for CIE, and did all the lettering for the headlines in the early issues of the magazine. In the later 1980s, she designed several typefaces with Arthur Baker that were released by her company AlphaOmega Typography. Hiroshige, released in 1986, was originally designed to premiere in a book designed by Hollandsworth, *One Hundred Famous Views of Edo* published by George Braziller Inc. The book presents woodblock prints by the nineteenth century Japanese artist Ando Hiroshige, thus the name of the typeface. The typeface Tiepolo was released by ITC in 1987. Both typefaces are based on written forms incorporating pen manipulation.

The use of the broad-edged pen gave an intrinsic relationship to the straight and curved parts of the early letterforms in the development of Hiroshige. However, subsequent (predigital) renderings of the letters were drawn. Interpreting these forms into a typeface required shoring up serifs and hairlines, cutting them in rubylith, and making photostats throughout the development cycle. At the end, says Hollandsworth "they were sculptural objects, which though completely based on pen shapes, were now 'drawn' letters suitable for the rigors of use in type." She has always been amused by the fact that once a designer publishes a typeface, there is no control over how others use it. For this exhibition, she gathered examples from one end of the spectrum to the other; Hiroshige used in art books of Japanese woodblock prints, and Hiroshige used in packaging for all-natural cream cheese. It is a measure of the success of a typeface to see it used in such a wide range of applications.

Through the 1990s, Hollandsworth managed typeface development, marketing and market research for the Agfa Corporation. She also became well known as an authority on the intellectual property protection of typefaces; she wrote numerous articles and lectured internationally on the topic. Hollandsworth is currently the Vice President of Operational Systems for Simon & Schuster Publishing, a division of Viacom.

All of the typefaces designed by AlphaOmega Typography were based on calligraphic renderings of the original letters. My partner at the time Hiroshige was designed in 1986 was Arthur Baker, well known for his innovative calligraphy books published by Dover and others. It was our feeling that all letterforms that derived from the Roman alphabet were most properly rendered with a broad-edged tool, manipulated on both the curves and straight strokes in the same way as the first century letters. C.H.

178

179

180

→ 178   Calligraphic heading for magazine.
        Reproduction of "Reader Survey" artwork for CIE.
        Example of pen lettering with manipulated strokes.
        Not dated. 5.5. x 6.25 inches.

→ 179   Calligraphic heading for magazine.
        Reproduction of "Q & A" artwork for CIE. Example of
        pen lettering with manipulated strokes. Not dated.
        5.5 x 5 inches.

→ 180   Calligraphic heading for magazine.
        Reproduction of "Classified" artwork for CIE. Outline
        drawing of pen lettering. Not dated. 5.5 x 7.75 inches.

  181   Page opening from *One Hundred Famous Views of Edo*.
        The typeface was created to premier in this book of
        Hiroshige's woodblock prints. Book design by Cynthia
        Hollandsworth. *One Hundred Famous Views of Edo.* George
        Braziller, New York, and the Brooklyn Museum, 1986.
        14.5 x 10 inches.

  182   Page opening from *Hiroshige: Birds and Flowers*.
        Set in a later version of Hiroshige by Linotype. Book
        design by Cynthia Hollandsworth. *Hiroshige: Birds
        and Flowers.* George Braziller, New York, in association
        with the Rhode Island School of Design, 1988.
        14.5 x 10 inches.

  183   Title for *National Parks*.
        Magazine using Hiroshige for titling. *National Parks*,
        Volume 75, Number 1-2, January–February 2001.
        10.75 x 8 inches.

  184   Packaging design.
        Hiroshige, used for cream cheese product name.
        Cabot Creamery, Cabot, Vermont. Not dated.
        2.75 x 4.75 x 1.25 inches.

  185   Untitled.
        Calligraphic broadside. Abstract composition in ink
        and gouache. 1989. 15.75 x 12.75 inches, framed.

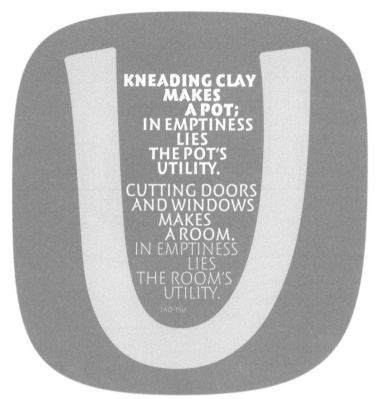

WOODLAND

→ 186 Woodland type specimen.
Specimen sheet with character settings for the light,
medium, demi and bold weights of Woodland. Typeface
is based on Akira Kobayashi's brush lettering. Released
by ITC in 1997. Type specimen designed by Akira
Kobayashi. Not dated. 11.75 x 8.25 inches.

Akira Kobayashi

Akira Kobayashi, of Japan, studied for four years at Musashino Art University in Tokyo, and later took calligraphy classes at the London College of Printing. He has many years of experience in both Japanese and Latin type production as a result of design positions he held at several Japanese firms. At Type Bank Company, Ltd., one of the leading type manufacturers in Japan, he designed Latin alphabets to accompany their seventeen Japanese digital fonts (kanji).

From 1997 to 2001, he devoted himself to working freelance in the area of Latin (western language) types. His designs include Luna, Japanese Garden, Scarborough, Seven Treasures, Silvermoon, Magnifico Daytime/Nighttime, Vineyard and Woodland for ITC; Acanthus and Clifford for FontShop International; Calcite for Adobe Systems; Conrad for Linotype Library GmbH; and Lithium for Typebox. His type designs have won awards in the 1996 Morisawa International Type Design Competition, the 1998 Upper & Lower Case Type Design Competition, the 1999 Kyrillitsa Design Competition, the 2000 Linotype Library International Digital Type Design Contest, and the 1998–2001 Type Directors Club Type Design Competitions. Kobayashi corresponds with Hermann Zapf and draws inspiration from the work of many western masters of typography and calligraphy. In 2001, he moved his family from Tokyo to Germany to accept a position as Type Director at Linotype Library GmbH in Bad Homburg.

His perspective and strength as a designer is to create Latin typefaces that may be used with or without kanji typefaces. Woodland, Clifford, and Acanthus all harmonize well with kanji typefaces, and demonstrate compatibility in weight, color, and texture. Kobayashi's design approach is rooted in the creation of classical Latin typographic and calligraphic forms that he often combines with his own stylized augmentations.

White spaces inside or between the letters are often more eloquent than black shapes. That is what I gained from Japanese calligraphy. It also applies to type design. A.K.

RECYCLE
Meltwater
RURAL SCENE
Environmental
MOSS-COVERED LIMBS
Ecological history written
GOLDEN HUES OF VINE MAPLE
Subtleties of form and function require

188

187 Woodland Light type specimen.
Type specimen showing character settings. Not dated.
9 x 8.25 inches.

→ 188 Woodland Medium type specimen.
Type specimen showing character settings. Not dated.
9 x 8.25 inches.

189 Woodland Demi type specimen.
Type specimen showing character settings. Not dated.
9 x 8.25 inches.

→ 190 Woodland Bold type specimen.
Type specimen showing character settings. Not dated.
9 x 8.25 inches.

191 Promotional brochure, with viola seed packet.
Set in Woodland Light, combined with a kanji typeface
for the Japanese text. Photographically illustrated.
Designed by Ryuichi Tateno for Zurich Life Insurance
Company, Ltd. Not dated. 4.25 x 8.25 inches, folded.

192 Promotional brochure, with petunia seed packet.
Set in Woodland Light, combined with a kanji typeface
for the Japanese text. Photographically illustrated.
Designed by Ryuichi Tateno for Zurich Life Insurance
Company, Ltd. Not dated. 4.25 x 8.25 inches, folded.

193 Page opening from *Druk*.
Title, headlines and text set in Woodland. Article about
Akira Kobayashi and his design work published in Dutch
typography trade magazine published by FontShop
Benelux. April 1999, Number 0. 12.25 x 6.5 inches.

→ 194 Calligraphic composition.
Quotation by Lao-Tsu, in English. Broadside designed
using paper-cut technique. Text arranged in alternating
lines of positive and negative images of uncial letterforms
and mounted on background paper. Not dated.
11.5 x 16.75 inches.

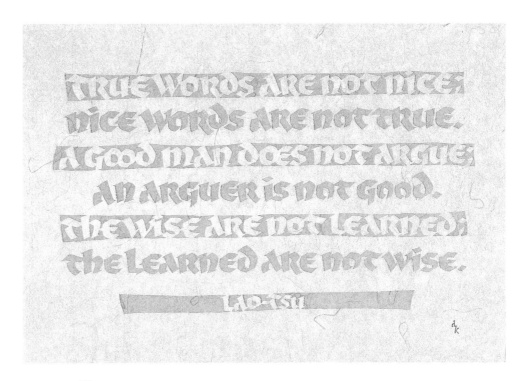

194

ITC WOODLAND HEAVY

NATURE
Resources
MUSHROOM
Ancient forest
ENRICHING THE SOIL
The legacy of a fallen log
KEEPING THE EARTH FERTILE
In every ecosystem, energy is trapped

190

195

HOFFMANN

→ 195 Hoffmann type specimen.
Richard Lipton based his type design on the lettering of calligrapher Lothar Hoffmann. Complete alphabets for each of the nine members of the type family appear in the border around the composition. Specimen design by Richard Lipton. Not dated. 16 x 14 inches.

Richard Lipton

Richard Lipton began his lettering career in 1974 as a calligrapher, sign painter and graphic designer, after studying art and design at Harpur College in upstate New York. Having established a successful freelance studio in Cambridge, Massachusetts, Lipton began work at Bitstream, the first independent digital type company. There, he digitized and renewed many classic and modern typefaces, adapting them to digital technologies. During his eight-year tenure as a senior designer at Bitstream, he developed two original type families, Cataneo (with Jacqueline Sakwa), and Arrus.

Since 1991, he has operated an independent type design and calligraphy studio. He designs original type for several foundries as well as custom fonts for international clients through Font Bureau. He continues to pursue calligraphy both commercially and for exhibition. His work has been shown internationally and has been featured in books and magazines. Lipton's other type designs include Alhambra, Avalon, Bremen, Ecru, Meno, Munich, Nutcracker, Shimano, Shogun, Sloop, and Talon, all for Font Bureau; and Bickham Script for Adobe Systems.

Lipton's calligraphic sensitivity and versatility is apparent in his type designs. He often draws inspiration from the example of lettering artists past and present. For example, the Hoffmann family was inspired by letters drawn and then cut out of paper by Michigan lettering artist, Lothar Hoffmann. Lipton expanded the concept and developed the family into four weights, from light to bold, each supported by an expert set, with separate black titling caps. His Avalon design was inspired by the work of Austrian calligrapher Friedrich Neugebauer. Bremen is an homage to the freehand poster capitals developed by lettering artist Ludwig Holwein in 1922. Ecru and Shogun were based on the inventive logos designed by Los Angeles graphic artist Margo Chase. Meno Roman and Italic were designed after studying the work of sixteenth century punchcutter Robert Granjon and seventeenth century master Dirk Voskens. Sloop owes its elegance to the classical scripts of Rhode Island calligrapher Raphael Boguslav. Bickham Script is based on the lettering of eighteenth century writing masters, as rendered in the engravings of George Bickham.

I came to type as a calligrapher. All that followed was destined to be influenced by the pen and brush. The shapes and textures of my type designs had no choice but to follow that more fluid path. R.L.

PHILOSOPHERS
BOLD
SCHOLARS INVESTIGATE TRUE MEANING OF LINT
BOLD EXPERT
DERIDE
BLACK TITLING
Machiavellian Schemes
ROMAN
BALLISTICS
LIGHT
INFANTRY EXERCISES INTERRUPTED BY HEAVY PRECIPITATION
BOOK EXPERT
BLIZZARD WATCH IN EFFECT
ROMAN
Thunderstorm
BOOK
WINDS REPORTED AT 326 MILES PER HOUR
LIGHT EXPERT
POLO MATCH MELEE
BLACK TITLING
Croquet match becomes a dirt-slinging, head-smashing free-for-all
LIGHT
Gauntlet
ROMAN

Richard Lipton designed the Hoffmann family from letters drawn and then cut out of paper as free-standing forms by contemporary Michigan lettering artist Lothar Hoffmann. Lipton follows creative development of contemporary lettering forms closely, searching for ideas that will yield type series. He digitized Hoffmann with Font Bureau in 1993, preparing four full weights, each supported by an expert set, plus a titling; FB 1993

9 STYLES: LIGHT, BOOK, ROMAN, AND BOLD, ALL WITH EXPERT, PLUS BLACK TITLING

196

→ 196 Hoffmann type specimen.
The nine fonts of the Hoffmann type family. The Font Bureau released Hoffmann in 1993. Specimen design by Tobias Frere-Jones, for Font Bureau's type specimen book. 1993. 10.5 x 7.25 inches.

We dance
to change
GHOST ourselves
DANCE Only when
SONG We have LEONARD
done this CROW
can we try DOG
to change
the Earth.

197 Hoffmann type specimen.
Text settings of the Hoffmann type family. Specimen design by Tobias Frere-Jones, for Font Bureau's type specimen book. 1993. 10.5 x 7.25 inches.

→ 198 *Ghost Dance Song.*
Calligraphic broadside. Text by Leonard Crow Dog. Calligraphy was electronically scanned and made into a print. Title and attribution hand lettered. Not dated. 15 x 10.5 inches.

CataneoLight/Swash/Extended
CataneoRegular/Swash/Extended
CataneoBold/Swash/Extended

Cataneo

LIGHT
ABCDEFGHIJKLMNOPQRSTUVWXYZ
abcdefghijklmnopqrstuvwxyz
0123456789⊖.,:;!?'$¢ÄÇÕÊÍÚ

REGULAR
ABCDEFGHIJKLMNOPQRSTUVWXYZ
abcdefghijklmnopqrstuvwxyz
0123456789⊖.,:;!?'$¢ÄÇÕÊÍÚ

BOLD
ABCDEFGHIJKLMNOPQRSTUVWXYZ
abcdefghijklmnopqrstuvwxyz
0123456789⊖.,:;!?'$¢ÄÇÕÊÍÚ

LIGHT SWASH
ABCDEFGHIJKLMNOPQRSTUVWXYZ
a d e g h k v p q r t v w y z
0123456789

REGULAR SWASH
ABCDEFGHIJKLMNOPQRSTUVWXYZ
a d e g h k v p q r t v w y z
0123456789

BOLD SWASH
ABCDEFGHIJKLMNOPQRSTUVWXYZ
a d e g h k v p q r t v w y z
0123456789

LIGHT EXTENDED
Ĺ Đ IJ Ę ¼¹/₄²/₃⁴/₅³/₈⁵/₈⁷/₈¹/₃²/₃ Ą Ŀ·LTh ff ffi ffl
ſⁿʒj ij ﬂ ﬆ ą ﬂ ﬆ đ ę ų & ſ

REGULAR EXTENDED
Ĺ Đ IJ Ę ¼¹/₄²/₃⁴/₅³/₈⁵/₈⁷/₈¹/₃²/₃ Ą Ŀ·LTh ff ffi ffl
ſⁿʒj ij ﬂ ﬆ ą ﬂ ﬆ đ ę ų & ſ

BOLD EXTENDED
Ĺ Đ IJ Ę ¼¹/₄²/₃⁴/₅³/₈⁵/₈⁷/₈¹/₃²/₃ Ą Ŀ·LTh ff ffi ffl
ſⁿʒj ij ﬂ ﬆ ą ﬂ ﬆ đ ę ų & ſ

CATANEO WAS DESIGNED FOR BITSTREAM AS A COLLABORATION BETWEEN RICHARD LIPTON AND JACKELINE SAKWA IN 1991-1992.

199

CATANEO

→ 199 Cataneo type specimen.
Typeface was designed in the spirit of the italic calligraphy of sixteenth century Italian writing master Bernardino Cataneo. Designed by Jacqueline Sakwa, in collaboration with Richard Lipton. Released by Bitstream in 1991–1992. Type specimen designed by Andrew Joslin. Not dated. 17 x 11 inches.

Jacqueline Sakwa

Jacqueline Sakwa earned a fine arts degree from the University of Massachusetts at Dartmouth in 1980, where she studied calligraphy and design with Howard Glasser. Thereafter, she joined the type drawing department at Compugraphic Corporation. She has worked as a freelance calligrapher and graphic designer throughout her type career, one of her primary clients being the publisher David R. Godine. She began working at Bitstream Inc., in 1982, shortly after it was established as the first independent digital type foundry, producing type on that company's proprietary computer design system. At Bitstream she worked under the direction of master type designer Matthew Carter, and with fellow calligrapher and type designer Richard Lipton.

In 1991–1992, Bitstream released Cataneo, an original type family designed by Jacqueline Sakwa and Richard Lipton. The Cataneo family has twelve styles that include three weights from Light to Bold, full sets of swash characters, ligatures, and accented characters. After eleven years helping to build Bitstream's library, Sakwa joined the Galapagos Design Group, where she was a consultant on type related projects. Sakwa recently received a masters degree in art education from the University of Massachusetts, and was certified as an art educator. She lives on the coast of Massachusetts, where she is also the art teacher at an elementary school. She has two sons and enjoys sea kayaking, gardening, and needlework.

For me, type was a natural extension of my interest in letterforms and graphic design. I don't believe that I would have been successful in my role as type designer without having the solid base I gained from calligraphy. In addition, it would not have been possible to understand the complexities of Bernardino Cataneo's work without having prior experience as a calligrapher. J.S.

202

206

200 Page opening from *An Italic Copybook*.
Facsimile of 1545 Renaissance manuscript written out
by Bernardino Cataneo. Sakwa studied this facsimile
for inspiration during the development of the typeface.
An Italic Copybook: The Cataneo Manuscript. Stephen
Harvard. Taplinger Publishing Company, New York,
1981. 9 x 10.5 inches.

201 Proof sheets for Cataneo swash capitals.
Computer print of regular weight characters. Tracing
paper overlay shows redrawing for the letter B. May 17,
1989. 11 x 51 inches.

→202 Proof sheet for Cataneo capitals.
Computer print of regular weight characters, with hand
drawn variations for the tail of the Q. Not dated.
8.5 x 11 inches.

203 Drawing for Cataneo swash letter.
Photocopy of enlarged letter with tracing paper overlay
showing redrawing in pencil. Not dated. 4.5 x 3.25 inches.

205

204 Drawing for Cataneo swash letter.
Outline drawing of capital letter, with points marked for
digitization. Not dated. 7 x 5.5 inches.

→ 205 Drawings for Cataneo swash W and M.
Studies for the development of swash capital letterforms.
Collage of original calligraphy, photocopies and an
outline drawing with points marked for digitization.
Not dated. 13.5 x 9.75 inches.

→ 206 Design for logo.
Quotation of a Latin proverb: *Nulla dies sine linea* (No day
without a line). Cataneo combined with calligraphic
figures. Commissioned by David R. Godine, Publisher,
Boston. 1995. 11 x 8.5 inches.

207 Book jacket for *The Velveteen Rabbit*.
The Velveteen Rabbit, or, How Toys Become Real. Margery
Williams. Illustrated by Ilse Plume. David R. Godine,
Boston, 1983. Calligraphy for title by Jacqueline Sakwa.
1983. 8.5 x 21 inches.

ABCDEFGHIJKLMNOPQRSTUVWX
YZ&1234567890abcdefghijklmnopqrstu
vwxyz&1234567890ABCDEFGHIJKLMNOP
QRSTUVWXYZ*ABCDEFGHIJKLMNOP*
QRSTUVWXYZ&1234567890ABCD
EFGHIJKLMNOPQRSTUVWX
YZabcdefghijklmnopqrstvwxyz 123456789

208

BRIOSO

→ 208 Brioso type specimen.
Detail from a specimen of text and display type family
based on Robert Slimbach's roman and italic calligraphy.
Specimen shows weights (light to bold) and optical
sizes (caption to display) and includes swash characters
and ornaments. Shown here are Regular Display roman
and italic. To be released by Adobe Systems in late 2001.
Type specimen designed by Robert Slimbach. 2001.
18 x 12 inches.

Robert Slimbach

Robert Slimbach began working in type design and calligraphy in 1983 when he was employed in the type drawing department of Autologic in Newbury Park, California. His early typefaces for ITC, Slimbach and Giovanni, marked the direction he would explore further when he joined Adobe Systems as one of their principal designers in 1987. Since that time his output has been prodigious, and he has designed a number of classically styled faces that are distinctive and widely used. He develops large, versatile text families, and is adept at utilizing the capabilities of multiple master and OpenType technologies in these designs. His typefaces routinely include typographic enhancements for many European languages, including Greek and Cyrillic. His ability to manage the design and technical details of thousands of characters in huge type families is akin to that of his Japanese colleagues who design types.

Slimbach draws inspiration from the great calligraphic and typographic masters of the past, as well as modern designers like Hermann Zapf and Gudrun Zapf von Hesse. His type families for Adobe include Brioso, Adobe Garamond, Adobe Jenson, Kepler, Cronos, Minion, Poetica, Sanvito, Utopia, Warnock, and Myriad (co-designed with Carol Twombly). Brioso reflects Slimbach's personal calligraphic style. It has the lively kinetics of his confident hand.

In 1991, Slimbach received the Charles Peignot Award from the Association Typographique Internationale for excellence in type design. His type designs and calligraphy have been exhibited internationally and featured in many design publications, including *Print* and *Letter Arts Review*. He lives in the heart of the Silicon Valley in Northern California, and is also a fine art photographer.

Through the years, the calligraphic lineage of our alphabet has repeatedly colored my type design work. After all, it is the direct connection between the pen and the human spirit that gives our alphabet its life and form. Hermann and Gudrun Zapf have always known this and remind the current generation that beauty can still be found in the products of our labor. R.S.

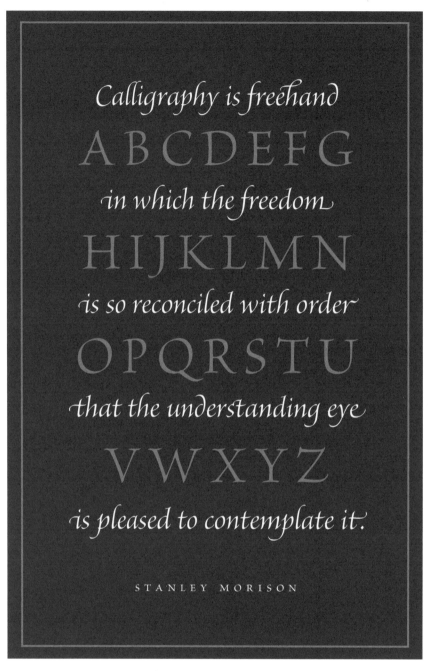

209

→ 209 Typographic composition.
Quotation by Stanley Morison set in Brioso Italic Display,
interlined with an alphabet set in Brioso Display capitals.
2001. 12.25 x 8 inches.

210 Sample text setting.
Sample text setting of Brioso, showing use in business
correspondence. 2001. 11 x 8.5 inches.

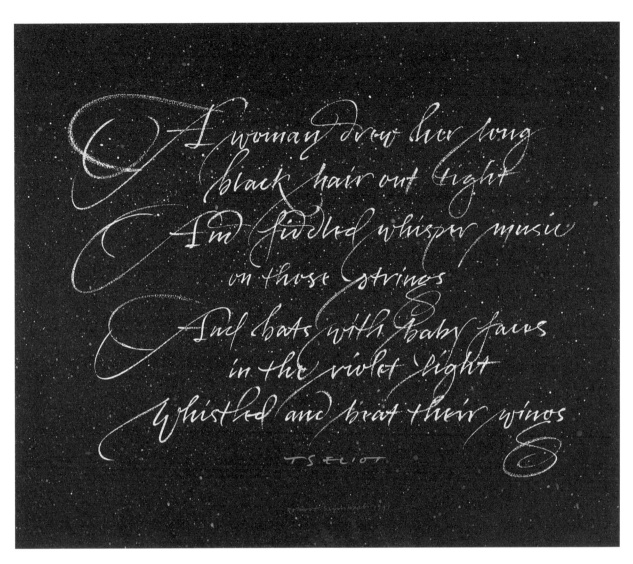

212

211 Jean Sibelius compact disk booklet.
Brioso Roman and Brioso Italic used in mock-up of
graphics for packaging. 2001. 5 x 5.5 inches.

→ 212 Calligraphic print.
Text from "The Wasteland," by T. S. Eliot.
Silkscreen print of brush-written calligraphy. 1991.
21 x 25.25 inches, framed.

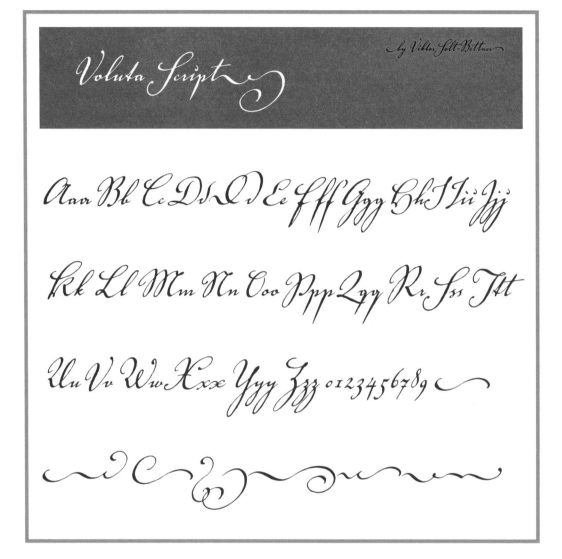

213

VOLUTA SCRIPT

→ 213 Voluta Script type specimen.
Script typeface with swashes and ornaments designed
to reflect Baroque architectural motifs. The typeface was
originally created for a project commissioned by the
Austrian Gallery at Castle Belvedere, Vienna. Released
by Adobe Systems in 1998. Type specimen designed by
Viktor Solt-Bittner. Not dated. 14 x 13 inches.

Viktor Solt-Bittner

Viktor Solt-Bittner lives and works in Vienna, Austria, where he studied graphic design at the Graphische Lehranstalt in the early 1990s. He has designed and released three typefaces: Voluta Script for Adobe Systems in 1998, Johann Sparkling for ITC in 1998, and Ballerino for ITC in 1999. In his developmental studies for these type designs, he researched calligraphic specimens from the eighteenth century, and then practiced writing these styles in his own hand until the shapes and rhythm of writing felt fluent and spontaneous. His lettering combines elements from both formal copperplate writing and informal *kurrent* handwriting of the eighteenth and nineteenth centuries. The resulting typefaces are a blend of historical styles with his own nuances. He characteristically likes to use rough contours, energetic swashes, and looping ascenders and descenders in his type designs. All these features are reminiscent of the traits seen in handwriting of both the eighteenth and the twenty first centuries.

Calligraphy has been my first contact to the world of graphic design and still makes a pleasant contrast to computer work. The computer is a wonderful means to correct errors in my calligraphic work and to make it more beautiful. Calligraphic type makes my calligraphy accessible to other designers. V. S-B.

Voluta Script was originally developed by Solt-Bittner for use in a children's guide to the Austrian Gallery in the Castle Belvedere in Vienna. The castle was the historic residence of Prince Eugene of Savoy, an eighteenth century military commander and art patron, and an important figure in Austrian history. A volute (in Latin, "voluta") is a spiral-shaped ornament used in the Baroque architecture of Prince Eugene's era. Solt-Bittner felt the *kurrent* writing of that time would appear illegible to modern readers, so he worked to produce clear letter shapes that retain an intricate Baroque essence.

Solt-Bittner uses his own handwriting and typefaces in his graphic design work, which includes commissions from book publishers and music compact disk publishers. He teaches calligraphy and typography at the University Fachhochschule Joanneum in Graz. While travelling back and forth by train between Vienna and Graz, he uses the time to work on his type designs.

Linotype v.51.8   Tue Apr 21 ✦ 31:16 PDT 1998

214 Handwriting exercise.
Print from scanned image of original writing. Exercises based on historic eighteenth century handwriting models were the first step in the development of Voluta Script. Not dated. 9 x 7 inches.

215 Voluta Script prototype.
Page from the proposal sent to Adobe Systems for development of Voluta Script. The working name of the typeface, Eugenius, appears on all developmental materials. November 4, 1997. 11 x 8.5 inches.

→ 216 Proof for Voluta Script.
Accent marks and accented capitals from series of proof prints. April 21, 1998. 11 x 8.5 inches.

216

219

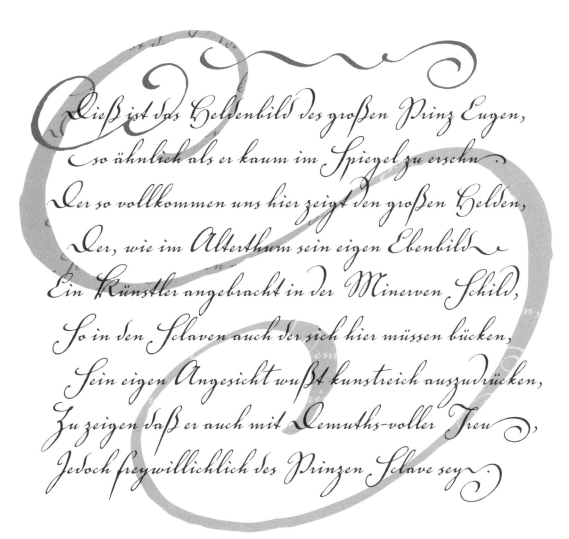

Dieß ist das Heldenbild des großen Prinz Eugen,
so ähnlich als er kaum im Spiegel zu ersehn.
Der so vollkommen uns hier zeigt den großen Helden,
Der, wie im Alterthum sein eigen Ebenbild
Ein Künstler angebracht in der Minerven Schild,
So in den Sclaven auch der sich hier müssen bücken,
Sein eigen Angesicht wußt kunstreich auszudrücken,
Zu zeigen daß er auch mit Demuths-voller Treu,
Jedoch freywillichlich des Prinzen Sclave sey.

222

217 Proof for Voluta Script capital A.
Outline drawing of accented character, from series of
final proofs. June 9, 1998. 11 x 8.5 inches.

218 Proof sheet for Voluta Script figures, fractions and signs.
From series of final proofs, marked with notes for
"tweaking" (refining) of the characters prior to release
of typeface. June 10, 1998. 11 x 8.5 inches.

→ 219 Design for compact disk booklet.
Artwork for packaging mock-up using Voluta Script.
Designed with decorative swashes and contrasting
pictographic illustrations. Not dated. 5 x 5.5 inches.

220 Design for Luca Monti compact disk booklet.
Packaging design in which Viktor Solt-Bittner combines
his calligraphy with type and photographic illustration.
Text on back cover of booklet reads: "Bach-Busoni,
Prokofieff, Liszt." Not dated. 5 x 5.5 inches.

221 Design for Salut d'Amour compact disk booklet.
Calligraphic title used for booklet design. Not dated.
5 x 5.5 inches.

→ 222 Untitled poem.
Poem in German about Prince Eugene of Savoy. Typo-
graphic composition set in Voluta Script and decorated
with Voluta Script swash ornaments. Designed by Viktor
Solt-Bittner for an exhibition in the Castle Belvedere,
Vienna. Not dated. 16 x 15.75 inches.

ABCDEF
GHIJKL
MNOPQ
RSTUV
WXYZabc
defghijklmno
pqrstuvwxyz
1234567890

Below: Full character set for
Ex Ponto.

ABCDEFGH
IJKLMNOP
QRSTUVWX
YZabcdefghijklm
nopqrstuvwxyz&
0123456789ÆŒ
ÞÐŁØ æœðłøfifl
ß‚ᵃº123$¢£¥ƒ¤/
¼½¾‰#°·^~<
>=–+¬÷×µ.,;:!?¡¿
‚''""„"———‹›«»()
[]{}|¦/_…†‡§
¢*.@©®™'ˆˇ˜
¨˙˝''„‚ÁÂÄÀ
ÅÃÇÉÊËÈÍÎ
ÏÌÑÓÔÖÒÕŠ
ÚÛÜÙÝŸŽáâ
äàåãçéêëèíîïìñóô
öòõšúûùüýÿž

223

EX PONTO

→ 223 Ex Ponto type specimen booklet.
Specimen of the capital and lowercase alphabets, with
figures, full character set and sample settings for alternate
and special characters. Illustrated here is one panel of
the page opening. Ex Ponto is based on Jovica Veljović's
handwritten letterforms. Released by Adobe Systems in
1995. 9 x 5.75 inches.

Jovica Veljović

Jovica Veljović earned a masters degree in calligraphy and lettering at the Academy of Applied Arts in Belgrade, Yugoslavia, where he also studied photography, printmaking, drawing, and painting. Since contemporary lettering resources were rare in Belgrade, he drew on the past for inspiration. He also corresponded with Henri Friedlaender, the eminent type designer and teacher from Jerusalem, who sent him Hermann Zapf's book, *About Alphabets*. It was this book that convinced Veljović that lettering and type design would become his own profession. He has since become a renowned calligrapher whose style is often characterized by expressive, rough-edged letters, fluidly written with graceful and lively spontaneity.

Veljović designed three type families for ITC in the 1980s: Veljović, Esprit, and Gamma. In 1985, he received the Charles Peignot Award from the Association Typographique Internationale for excellence in calligraphy and type design. He has taught calligraphy workshops around the world, as well as classes at the Academy in Belgrade where he earned his degree. In 1992, when Yugoslavia became embroiled in civil war, he left Belgrade with his family to begin a new life in Germany. Since then, he has been teaching type design and calligraphy at the Fachhochschule Hamburg.

What is fascinating to me about Hermann Zapf's letterforms is not their virtuosity but their elegance. I admire his refined sense of form and his way of combining the elements of typography, paper, and binding in his book designs. In his work I see poetry, sincerity, and beauty of form that have never been seen before. This has become my ideal, too. J.V.

It was during his initial years in Germany that Veljović began designing Ex Ponto, his first typeface for Adobe Systems. This type family is based on his personal style of calligraphic writing with a Brause 505 pen nib. He began the design by writing calligraphic characters on rough paper and then modifying these ragged-edged letterforms on the computer to produce a graceful, balanced typeface. Ex Ponto was released in 1995 as a multiple master type family with one axis for weights from light to bold.

In 2000, Adobe released his OpenType family, Silentium, which is based on tenth century Carolingian writing. Veljović has also designed a typeface for the exclusive use of the German newspaper *Die Zeit*, and he has served as a consultant on Cyrillic type designs for Apple Computer, Inc., Linotype Library GmbH, and URW Software & Type. His work has been published in many books and magazines, including *Letter Arts Review, Print*, and *Hamburger Satzspiegel*.

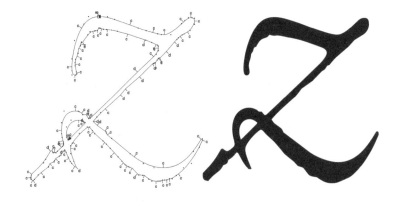

Ex Ponto has an alternating rough and smooth outer contour, reflecting what actually happens to pen strokes on rough paper. To produce this rough edge on the computer, Veljović placed hundreds of Bézier points strategically on each character of the typeface. The Z, for example, has 95 Bézier elements defining its contour, including both curves and straight lines.

224

→ 224 Detail from Ex Ponto type specimen booklet. Reproductions of calligraphic studies for the typeface and illustration of the digitization process for the character Z. 1995. 9 x 5.75 inches.

Die Schwierigkeiten wachsen je näher man dem Ziele kommt.

GOETHE

225

→ 225 New Year's greeting card. Quotation by Goethe, "The difficulties grow the nearer one comes to the goal." Reproduction of calligraphy for personal greeting card. 1993. 4.25 x 8.25 inches, folded.

FRANCIS BACON · OF BEAUTY

229

226 *Schrift kommt vom Schreiben* (type comes from writing).
Two-page display of Ex Ponto in a German typographic
trade journal. Reproduction of text by Thomas Carlyle
illustrates the calligraphic basis for the typeface. Specimen
of Ex Ponto is set with a text by Ivo Andrić. Published in
Hamburger Satzspiegel, Hamburg. January 1995.
16.5 x 11.75 inches.

227 Book cover for *Other Chinas*.
Ex Ponto used for the title of book. *Other Chinas*. Ralph
A. Litzinger. Durham, North Carolina, Duke University
Press, 2000. 9.25 x 6 inches.

228 Brochure for Asian Art Museum, San Francisco.
Ex Ponto used for titling on brochure. Not dated.
9 x 4 inches, folded.

→ 229 *Of Beauty.*
Original calligraphy. Text by Francis Bacon. Red and
black ink on paper. 2001. 15 x 20 inches.

230

WATERS TITLING

→ 230   Waters Titling type specimen.
Laser print showing the different weights of the alphabets
and figures in the typeface. Waters Titling is a display
family based on Julian Waters's pen-made roman capitals.
Released by Adobe Systems as a multiple master font in
1997. Type specimen designed by Julian Waters. Not
dated. 11 x 8.5 inches.

Julian Waters

Julian Waters grew up amidst calligraphy and fine books. The square-edged pen nib must have been as familiar to him as the spoon was to other children. His British parents, Sheila and Peter Waters, have long been important figures in their respective fields of calligraphy, bookbinding, and book conservation. His first calligraphy teacher was his mother Sheila Waters, but in 1979 he began intensive study with Hermann Zapf, in the annual master calligraphy class held at the Rochester Institute of Technology in New York. Over the next decade he returned for further study and instruction with Professor Zapf, and in 1989 succeeded him as instructor of the master class. His calligraphy, naturally enough, echoes some traits of the Zapf style, with its graceful roman capitals, fluid italic swashes, and strong and sure blackletter. Nevertheless, Waters's style is distinctive and personal.

Waters is sought after for his commercial design and lettering work, and his clients include the National Geographic Society, the U. S. Postal Service, book publishers and telecommunications companies. He taught calligraphy and graphic design for several years at the Corcoran College of Art in Washington, D.C., and he travels frequently to teach calligraphy workshops and to lecture throughout North America, Europe, and Asia. His work is represented in almost every contemporary book on calligraphy. Awards include recognition from the Type Directors Club, the Art Directors Club, *Print,* and *Letter Arts Review.* Waters's personal artistic endeavors involve combining traditional tools – brushes, pens, and papers – with contemporary tools and devices such as copier machines and digital printers.

Adobe Systems released the Waters Titling family in 1997. It is a two-axis multiple master typeface in a range of weights from light to bold, and in widths from condensed to normal. Swash alternate characters, ligatures, and a "tall cap" variant are included in the character sets. The typeface is clearly informed by two thousand year-old Roman monumental inscription letters, but it also has the contemporary flair of his own distinctive pen and brush-made roman capitals.

Waters lives in Gaithersburg, Maryland with his daughters and his wife Cathy, who is also an accomplished calligrapher and illustrator.

As a child in England I was continually intrigued as I watched the ink flow through the pen of my mother, Sheila. After moving to the U. S. as a teenager, I became increasingly fascinated by the lettering arts. For me the work of Gudrun and Hermann Zapf became supreme benchmarks of taste, sophistication and fitness for purpose. I was fortunate to study with Hermann Zapf several times, starting in 1979. My efforts in type design are a natural outgrowth of my pen lettering work. The formal multi-weight family Waters Titling follows in the tradition of pen inspired type design so nobly expressed in their work. J.W.

![Waters Titling type specimen showing swash capitals, ligatured letters, and alternate characters on a marble background]

S ES ST KS
ZA EA EY Y
K K KE E
CT CA TY
R R R RS

A few of the swash characters, ligatures
and alternates comprising the new typeface

WATERS TITLING CAPITALS

designed by Julian Waters
for Adobe Systems Inc

232

234

231 Waters Titling type specimen.
Laser print showing different weights and widths of
the type, ligatures and "tag words" (word ligatures).
Type specimen designed by Julian Waters. Not dated.
11 x 8.5 inches.

→ 232 Waters Titling type specimen.
Laser print showing swash capitals, ligatured letters,
and alternate characters. Type specimen designed by
Julian Waters. Not dated. 11 x 8.5 inches.

233 Announcement card for the Sidwell Friends School,
Washington, D.C.
Printed card, designed using Waters Titling for
highlighted information and initials in text. 1997.
7 x 10 inches.

If I were asked to say
what is at once the most important
production of Art and the thing
most to be longed for, I should answer

A BEAUTIFUL HOUSE

and if I were further asked to name
the production next in importance
and the thing next to be longed for
I should answer

A BEAUTIFUL BOOK

To enjoy good houses and good books
in self respect and decent comfort
seems to me to be the pleasurable end
towards which all societies
of human beings   WILLIAM MORRIS
ought now to struggle

235

→ 234   *Wisdom: Proverbs 19:20.*
        Text from the Bible, Proverbs 19:20. Reproduction of
        calligraphy, scanned and printed on a matte finish heavy
        weight archival paper with an Epsom 1270 color printer.
        Originally designed as a commission for Gibson
        Greetings. 2001. 13.5 x 13 inches.

→ 235   *Beautiful House.*
        Text by William Morris. Reproduction of calligraphic
        broadside originally created in 1996. Not dated.
        19 x 13 inches.

236   *Spontaneous alphabet.*
      Reproduction of calligraphy. The original calligraphy
      was spontaneously written as a workshop demonstration.
      Printed in black on gold background. 2000.
      15.5 x 11 inches.

Selected Bibliography

TYPOGRAPHY

Baskin, Leonard. *Zapf's Civilité Disclosed: Adorned with Terse and Pithy Apothegms.* [Northampton, Massachusetts]: Gehenna Press, 1995.

Baudin, Fernand. *How Typography Works (And Why It Is Important).* New York: Design Press, 1988.

Bigelow, Charles, Paul Hayden Duensing, and Linnea Gentry, eds. *Fine Print on Type: The Best of Fine Print Magazine on Type and Typography.* San Francisco: Bedford Arts, 1989.

Blackwell, Lewis. *Twentieth Century Type: Remix.* Corte Madera, California: Gingko Press, 1998.

Blumenthal, Joseph. *Art of the Printed Book 1455–1955: Masterpieces of Typography Through Five Centuries from the Collections of the Pierpont Morgan Library.* New York: Pierpont Morgan Library; Boston: David R. Godine, 1973.

Brancyk, Alexander, et al., eds. *Emotional_Digital: A Sourcebook of Contemporary Typographics.* London: Thames & Hudson, 1999.

Bringhurst, Robert. *The Elements of Typographic Style.* 2d ed. Point Roberts, Washington: Hartley & Marks, 1996.

Carter, John, and Percy H. Muir, eds. *Printing and the Mind of Man: A Descriptive Catalogue Illustrating the Impact of Print on the Evolution of Western Civilization During Five Centuries.* London: Cassell and Company; New York: Holt, Rinehart & Winston, 1967.

Carter, Sebastian. *Twentieth Century Type Designers.* New ed. New York: W. W. Norton, 1995.

Chappell, Warren. *A Short History of the Printed Word.* Boston: Nonpareil Books, 1980.

Dowding, Geoffrey. *An Introduction to the History of Printing Types: An Illustrated Summary of the Main Stages in the Development of Type Design from 1440 Up to the Present Day: An Aid to Type Face Identification.* London: British Library; New Castle, Delaware: Oak Knoll Press, 1998.

Dreyfus, John. *Into Print: Selected Writings on Printing History, Typography and Book Production.* Boston: David R. Godine, 1995.

Dreyfus, John. *The Work of Jan van Krimpen: A Record in Honour of His Sixtieth Birthday.* Haarlem: Johannes Enschedé en Zonen, 1952.

Febvre, Lucien and Henri-Jean Martin. *The Coming of the Book: The Impact of Printing, 1450–1800.* London: Verso, 1984.

Friedl, Friedrich, Nicholaus Ott, and Bernard Stein. *Typography: An Encyclopedic Survey of Type Design and Techniques Throughout History.* New York: Black Dog & Leventhal, 1998.

Goudy, Frederic W. *Goudy's Type Designs: His Story and Specimens.* 2d ed. New Rochelle, New York: Myriade Press, 1978.

Grannis, Chandler B., ed. *Heritage of the Graphic Arts: A Selection of Lectures Delivered at Gallery 303, New York City Under the Direction of Dr. Robert L. Leslie.* New York: R. R. Bowker, 1972.

Heller, Steven, and Philip B. Meggs. *Texts on Type: Critical Writings on Typography.* New York: Allworth Press, 2001.

Johnson, A. F. *Selected Essays on Books and Printing.* Edited by Percy H. Muir. Amsterdam: Van Gendt, 1970.

Johnson, A. F. *Type Designs: Their History and Development.* 3rd ed., new and rev. London: Deutsch, 1966.

Kapr, Albert. *Johann Gutenberg: The Man and His Invention.* Translated by Douglas Martin. Aldershot, England: Scolar Press; Brookfield, Vermont: Ashgate, 1996.

Karow, Peter. *Digital Formats for Typefaces.* Hamburg: URW, 1987.

Kinross, Robin. *Modern Typography: An Essay in Critical History.* London: Hyphen Press, 1992.

Klingspor, Karl. *Über Schönheit von Schrift und Druck.* Frankfurt am Main: George Kurt Schaur, 1949.

Knuttel, Gerard. *The Letter as a Work of Art: Observations and Confrontations with Contemporaneous Expressions of Art from Roman Times to the Present Day.* Amsterdam: Lettergieterij "Amsterdam" Voorheen N. Tetterode, 1951.

Lawson, Alexander. *Anatomy of a Typeface.* Boston: David R. Godine, 1990.

Lewis, John. *Anatomy of Printing: The Influences of Art and History on Its Design.* New York: Watson-Guptill Publications, 1970.

Lewis, John. *The Twentieth Century Book: Its Illustration and Design.* 2d ed. New York: Van Nostrand Reinhold, 1984.

McGrew, Mac. *American Metal Typefaces of the Twentieth Century.* 2nd revised ed. New Castle, Delaware: Oak Knoll Press, 1993.

McLean, Ruari. *The Thames and Hudson Manual of Typography.* London: Thames & Hudson, 1980.

Macrakis, Michael S. *Greek Letters: From Tablets to Pixels.* New Castle, Delaware: Oak Knoll Press, 1996.

Meggs, Philip B. *A History of Graphic Design.* 3rd ed. New York: John Wiley & Sons, 1998.

Morison, Stanley. *Letter Forms: Typographic and Scriptorial; Two Essays on Their Classification, History and Bibliography.* New York: Typophiles, 1968.

Morison, Stanley. *Selected Essays on the History of Letter Forms in Manuscript and Print*. Edited by David McKitterick. 2 vols. Cambridge: Cambridge University Press, 1981.

Morison, Stanley, and Kenneth Day. *The Typographic Book, 1450–1935: A Study of Fine Typography Through Five Centuries*. Chicago: University of Chicago Press, 1963.

Morison, Stanley, and Holbrook Jackson. *A Brief Survey of Printing: History and Practice*. New York: Alfred A. Knopf, 1923.

Morris, William. *The Ideal Book: Essays and Lectures on the Arts of the Book*. Edited by William Peterson. Berkeley and Los Angeles: University of California Press, 1982.

Noordzij, Gerrit. *Letterletter: An Inconsistent Collection of Tentative Theories That Do Not Claim Any Other Authority Than That of Common Sense*. Point Roberts, Washington: Hartley & Marks, 2000.

Rosarivo, Raúl M. *Divina Proportio Typographica*. Krefeld, Germany: Scherpe, 1961.

Sassoon, Rosemary. *Computers and Typography*. Oxford: Intellect, 1993.

Schmets, Ronald. *Vom Schriftgiessen: Porträt der Firma D. Stempel, Frankfurt am Main*. Darmstadt: Technische Hochschule Darmstadt, 1987.

Spiekermann, Erik, and E. M. Ginger. *Stop Stealing Sheep and Find Out How Type Works*. Mountain View, California: Adobe Press, 1993.

Stauffacher, Jack Werner. *A Typographic Journey: The History of the Greenwood Press and Bibliography, 1934–2000*. San Francisco: Book Club of California, 1999.

Steinberg, S. H. *Five Hundred Years of Printing*. New ed. London: British Library; New Castle, Delaware: Oak Knoll Press, 1996.

Stone, Sumner. *On Stone: The Art and Use of Typography on the Personal Computer*. San Francisco: Bedford Arts, 1991.

Sutton, James and Alan Bartram. *An Atlas of Typeforms*. New York: Hastings House, 1968.

Tracy, Walter. *Letters of Credit: A View of Type Design*. Boston: David R. Godine, 1986.

Tschichold, Jan. *The Form of the Book: Essays on the Morality of Good Design*. Translated by Hajo Hadeler. Edited by Robert Bringhurst. Point Roberts, Washington: Hartley & Marks, 1991.

Twenty Years of the Frederic W. Goudy Award. Rochester, New York: Press of the Good Mountain, 1988.

Updike, Daniel Berkeley. *Printing Types: Their History, Forms, and Use; A Study in Survivals*. 3rd ed. 2 vols. Cambridge, Massachusetts: Belknap Press, 1962.

Van Krimpen, Jan. *On Designing and Devising Type*. New York: Typophiles, 1957.

Vervliet, Hendrik D. L., ed. *The Book Through Five Thousand Years: A Survey*. London: Phaidon, 1972.

Warde, Beatrice. *The Crystal Goblet: Sixteen Essays on Typography*. Selected and edited by Henry Jacob. Cleveland: World, 1956.

Wilson, Adrian. *The Design of Books*. San Francisco: Chronicle Books, 1993.

Young, Doyald. *Fonts and Logos: Font Analysis, Logotype Design, Typography, Type Comparison, and History*. Sherman Oaks, California: Delphi Press, 1999

CALLIGRAPHY

Anderson, Donald M. *The Art of Written Forms: The Theory and Practice of Calligraphy*. New York: Holt, Rinehart & Winston, 1969.

Benson, John Howard, and Arthur Graham Carey. *The Elements of Lettering*. 2d ed. New York: McGraw-Hill, 1950.

Brinkley, John, ed. *Lettering Today: A Survey and Reference Book*. London: Studio Vista, 1964.

Child, Heather. *Calligraphy Today: Twentieth-Century Tradition and Practice*. New York: Taplinger, 1988.

Cinamon, Gerald. *Rudolf Koch: Letterer, Type Designer, Teacher*. New Castle, Delaware: Oak Knoll Press; London: British Library, 2000.

Contemporary Calligraphy: Modern Scribes and Lettering Artists II. New York: Taplinger, 1986.

Diringer, David. *The Hand-Produced Book*. London: Hutchinson's Scientific & Technical Publications, 1953.

Fairbank, Alfred. *A Book of Scripts*. Harmondsworth, England: Penguin, 1949.

Gaur, Albertine. *A History of Writing*. London: British Library, 1984.

Gray, Nicolete. *A History of Lettering: Creative Experiment and Letter Identity*. Boston: David R. Godine, 1986.

Harris, David. *Calligraphy: Modern Masters – Art, Inspiration, and Technique*. New York: Crescent Books, 1991.

Harvard, Stephen. *An Italic Copybook: The Cataneo Manuscript*. New York: Taplinger, 1981.

Harvey, Michael. *Creative Lettering Today: Calligraphy in the Graphic Arts: Drawing and Design, Digital Letterforms, Carving Letters in Stone and Wood*. New York: Design Books, 1996.

Hayes, James. *The Roman Letter*. Chicago: Lakeside Press, 1952.

Hoffmann, Herbert, and Alfred Finsterer. *Hoffmanns Schriftatlas: Ausgewählte Alphabete und Anwendungen aus Vergangenheit und Gegenwart*. Stuttgart: Julius Hoffmann, 1952.

International Calligraphy Today. New York: Watson-Guptill Publications, 1982.

Jackson, Donald. *The Story of Writing*. London: Studio Vista, 1981.

Jensen, Hans. *Sign, Symbol and Script: An Account of Man's Efforts to Write*. New York: G. P. Putnam's Sons, 1969.

Johnston, Edward. *Writing and Illuminating and Lettering*. London: A. C. Black; New York: Taplinger, 1977.

Johnston, Priscilla. *Edward Johnston*. London: Faber & Faber, 1959.

Kapr, Albert. *The Art of Lettering: The History, Anatomy, and Aesthetics of the Roman Letter Forms*. New York: K. G. Saur, 1983.

Knight, Stan. *Historical Scripts: From Classical Times to the Renaissance*. New Castle, Delaware: Oak Knoll Press, 1998.

Knuth, Donald. E. *3:16 Bible Texts Illuminated*. Madison, Wisconsin: A-R Editions, 1990.

Koch, Rudolf. *Das Schreibbüchlein*. Translated by Barbara Thompson. Kassel: Johannes Stauda Verlag, 1984.

Koch, Rudolf. *Das Schreiben als Kunstfertigkeit; Eine ausführliche Anleitung zur Erlernung der für den Beruf des Schreibers notwendigen Schriftarten*. Leipzig: Deutschen Buchgewerbe-Vereins, 1921.

Koch, Rudolf. *The Little ABC Book of Rudolf Koch*. Boston: David R. Godine; London: Merrion Press, 1976.

Lindegren, Erik. *ABC of Lettering and Printing Types*. 3 vols. New York: Museum Books, 1964.

Macdonald, Byron J. *The Art of Lettering with the Broad Pen*. New York: Reinhold, 1966.

Mediavilla, Claude. *Calligraphy: From Calligraphy to Abstract Painting*. Translated by Alan Marshall. Wommelgem, Belgium: Scirpus, 1996.

Morison, Stanley. *Politics and Script: Aspects of Authority and Freedom in the Development of Graeco-Latin Script from the Sixth Century B.C. to the Twentieth Century A.D.; The Lyell Lectures 1957*. Edited and completed by Nicolas Barker. Oxford: Clarendon Press, 1972.

Osley, A. S., ed. *Calligraphy and Palaeography: Essays Presented to Alfred Fairbank on His 70th Birthday*. London: Faber & Faber, 1965.

Three Classics of Italian Calligraphy: An Unabridged Reissue of the Writing Books of Arrighi, Tagliente, and Palatino. With an Introduction by Oscar Ogg. New York: Dover, 1953.

Tschichold, Jan. *Treasury of Alphabets and Lettering: A Source Book of the Best Letter Forms of Past and Present for Sign Painters, Graphic Artists, Commercial Artists, Typographers, Printers, Sculptors, Architects, and Schools of Art and Design*. New York: Reinhold, 1966.

Two Thousand Years of Calligraphy: A Three-Part Exhibition Organized by The Baltimore Museum of Art, Peabody Institute Library, Walters Art Gallery June 6–July 18, 1965. Baltimore: Walters Art Gallery, 1965.

Wardrop, James. *The Script of Humanism: Some Aspects of Humanistic Script: 1460–1560*. Oxford: Clarendon Press, 1963.

Whalley, Joyce Irene. *The Pen's Excellencie: Calligraphy of Western Europe and America*. New York: Taplinger, 1980.

Woodcock, John. *A Book of Formal Scripts*. Boston: David R. Godine, 1993.

PUBLICATIONS: HERMANN ZAPF

ABC-XYZapf: Fifty Years in Alphabet Design: Professional and Personal Contributions Selected for Hermann Zapf. Edited by John Dreyfus and Knut Erichson. London: Wynkyn de Worde Society; Offenbach: Bund Deutscher Buchkünstler, 1989.

About Alphabets. Some Marginal Notes on Type Design. New York: Typophiles, 1960.

About Alphabets. Some Marginal Notes on Type Design. Cambridge, Massachusetts and London: MIT Press, 1970.

August Rosenberger 1893–1980: A Tribute to One of the Great Masters of Punchcutting, an Art Now All but Extinct. Rochester, New York: Privately Printed by the Melbert B. Cary, Jr. Graphic Arts Collection, Rochester Institute of Technology, 1996.

Creative Calligraphy: Instructions and Alphabets; A New Instruction Manual for Learning the Art of Calligraphy. Translated by Stephen Morton and Paul Standard. West Germany: Rotringwerke Riepe KG, 1985.

The Fine Art of Letters: The Work of Hermann Zapf: Exhibited at the Grolier Club, New York, 2000. New York: Grolier Club, 2000.

Hermann Zapf and His Design Philosophy: Selected Articles and Lectures on Calligraphy and Contemporary Developments in Type Design, with Illustrations and Bibliographical Notes, and a Complete List of His Typefaces. Chicago: Society of Typographic Arts, 1987.

Hermann Zapf: Ein Arbeitsbericht. Hamburg: Maximilian-Gesellschaft, 1984.

Manuale Typographicum. New York: Museum Books,1954.

Manuale Typographicum: One Hundred Typographical Arrangements with Considerations About Types, Typography and the Art of Printing Selected from Past and Present, Printed in Eighteen Languages. Frankfurt: Z-Presse; New York: Museum Books, 1968.

"The Art of Hermann Zapf," in *Zapfino*. Linotype Library compact disk CD909DEF1.0. Short film originally produced by Hallmark Cards, Inc., Kansas City, Missouri.

Orbis Typographicus: Thoughts, Words and Phrases on the Arts and Sciences. Prairie Village, Kansas: Crabgrass Press, 1980.

Pen and Graver: Alphabets and Pages of Calligraphy. New York: Museum Books, 1952.

Poetry Through Typography. New York: Kelly/Winterton Press, 1993.

Sammlung Hermann Zapf, Herzog August Bibliothek, Wolfenbüttel. Wolfenbüttel: Herzog August Bibliothek, 1993.

Typographic Variations, Designed by Hermann Zapf on Themes in Contemporary Book Design and Typography in 78 Book- and Title-Pages. New York: Museum Books, 1964.

Zapf, Hermann, and John Dreyfus. *Classical Typography in the Computer Age: Papers Presented at a Clark Library Seminar 27 February 1988*. Los Angeles: William Andrews Clark Memorial Library, University of California, Los Angeles, 1991.

Zapf, Hermann, and August Rosenberger. *Das Blumen-ABC*. Frankfurt am Main: D. Stempel, 1962.

Zapf, Hermann, and Jack Werner Stauffacher. *Hunt Roman: The Birth of a Type*. Pittsburgh: Pittsburgh Bibliophiles, 1965.

Hallmark Uncial. Type design by Hermann Zapf for Hallmark Cards, Inc. 1970. Quotation by Quintus Horatius Flaccus: "giving pleasure to the reader at the same time as instruction." Specimen setting by Rick Cusick.

Contributors to the Catalogue

RICK CUSICK is one of America's foremost calligraphers. Born in 1947 in Stockton, California, and interested in letters since childhood, he first studied calligraphy with James R. Lewis at San Joaquin Delta College. After graduation, he worked at Ad/Art, Inc., designing illuminated signs, before attending Art Center College of Design in Los Angeles. Recruited by Hallmark Cards in 1971, he continues to be employed there as a designer in the lettering and book departments. He taught editorial publication design at the University of Kansas, and has been the art director of *Letter Arts Review* since 1992. In addition to his work in original lettering and design, Cusick has designed a number of proprietary typefaces for Hallmark, as well as the Nyx typeface for Adobe. For many years Cusick corresponded with veteran calligraphers of the generation preceding his own, including Ray DaBoll, James Hayes, Maury Nemoy, Father Edward M. Catich, and Lloyd Reynolds. In tribute to three of these important figures, he compiled, edited and designed *With Respect...to RFD,* on Raymond F. DaBoll, *Straight Impressions,* on Lloyd Reynolds, and *OK? It's all Yours! Informal Recollections of Arnold Bank.* He also collaborated with the late Warren Chappell to produce *The Proverbial Bestiary.* Cusick is currently a Lettering Studio Manager at Hallmark with responsibilities that include font development.

JERRY KELLY is a typographer, printer, and calligrapher. He worked as a designer and representative for The Stinehour Press from 1991 to 1999. Prior to that, he was a designer and director of typography and design for A. Colish, Inc., Mount Vernon, New York. As a partner in the Kelly/Winterton Press since 1978, he uses hand-set type and letterpress printing to produce books and ephemera for a variety of clients. He also works as a freelance calligrapher for commercial clients and book publishers. As a designer of books and other print materials he produces work for many museums and institutions, including The Library of America, Rochester Institute of Technology, The Morgan Library, Columbia University, and The Grolier Club. He has taught and lectured on calligraphy, typography, and printing at the Parsons School of Design, the Pratt Institute in New York, Camberwell College in London, and at Stanford University and Scripps College in California. The author of numerous articles, he has also curated several exhibitions on typography and calligraphy. A 1978 graduate of Queens College, City University of New York, he attended Hermann Zapf's summer master classes in calligraphy at RIT between 1979 and 1987.

LINNEA LUNDQUIST grew up in Maine with seven brothers and sisters. She earned her undergraduate degree from the School of Printing at the Rochester Institute of Technology, where several teachers of calligraphy and typography, including Hermann Zapf, influenced her. She then served in the U. S. Army, jumping out of airplanes, supervising burial ceremonies, and designing engineer training manuals before departing, in 1984, with the rank of captain. She was a graduate student in the book arts at Mills College in Oakland, California, and studied Printing History at the Library Science School at the University of California at Berkeley. In 1990, she joined the type design and production staff at Adobe Systems in San Jose, California, where she continues to work on the development of the Adobe Originals type library. Since 1988, she has also been a partner with blackletter calligrapher Ward Dunham in Atelier Gargoyle, a letterpress and calligraphy studio in San Francisco. Her first type design won the Silver Prize in the Morisawa International Type Design Competition in 1999. To enhance her typographic vocation, she continues to study calligraphy. She organized the Zapfest exhibition because of her love of calligraphy, type design, and books, and in appreciation of the work of Hermann and Gudrun Zapf.

JOHN PRESTIANNI trained as a calligrapher with David Mekelburg at Immaculate Heart College in Los Angeles. He later studied with Ann Camp at Digby Stuart College of the Sacred Heart in London, where, in 1979, he was elected a Fellow of the Society of Scribes and Illuminators. He worked as a designer in book and magazine publishing for many years, and, as a freelance lettering artist, produced calligraphy for a wide variety of purposes. He was the founding editor of *Alphabet, The Journal of the Friends of Calligraphy,* and has written about calligraphy, typography and related topics, including a biographical treatment on Hermann Zapf. His lettering and calligraphy have been published in *Calligraphy Today: Twentieth-Century Tradition and Practice, The Calligrapher's Handbook, Modern Scribes and Lettering Artists, Painting for Calligraphers, The Craft of Calligraphy,* and other publications.

JACK STAUFFACHER is well known as a printer, typographer and teacher of book design and the history of printing. Born in 1920, he founded The Greenwood Press in 1934, which he continues to operate at its current location at 300 Broadway in San Francisco. He lived and studied in Florence, Italy, as a Fulbright

Scholar from 1955 to 1958. Following that, he was Assistant Professor of Typographic Design at the Carnegie Institute of Technology in Pittsburgh from 1959 to 1963. There, he founded and directed the New Laboratory Press, which succeeded Porter Garnett's Laboratory Press. During this time, he invited Hermann Zapf to teach a six-week seminar on book design and lettering. This led to Zapf's design of Hunt Roman for the Hunt Botanical Library. Between 1964 and 1969 he was Typographic Director at the Stanford University Press and taught part-time at the San Francisco Art Institute. He held a Regent's Professorship at the University of California at Santa Cruz in 1974, where he later established the Cowell Press. In 1982 he taught at the Book Arts Institute at the University of Alabama, Tuscaloosa. He has lectured widely, including at such institutions as Yale University, the Rochester Institute of Technology, Southern Methodist University, Princeton University, Northwestern University and the American Institute of Graphic Arts. He was a consultant in typography for Adobe Systems in 1986, at the invitation of Sumner Stone. In 1991, he and Hermann Zapf were invited to be members of the International Jury for the Book Design Award for the Biennale Felice Feliciano, in Verona, Italy (in which he has twice been a finalist). More than one commentator has characterized him as the leading American exponent of the minimalist style of printing associated with the Swiss typographer Jan Tschichold. Stauffacher's publications include *Janson: A Definitive Collection* (1954); *Albert Camus – The Rebel: Twenty-Five Typographic Meditations* (1969), a portfolio of typographic broadsides employing large wooden type letters; *Phaedrus, a dialogue by Plato* (1978); *Nicholas Kis: Hungarian Punchcutter and Printer: 1650–1702* (1983); *The Horace Odes* (1990); *Porter Garnett, Philosophical Writings on the Ideal Book* (1994); and *A typographic Journey: the History of The Greenwood Press and Bibliography, 1934–2000* (2000).

SUMNER STONE is the principal and founder of Stone Type Foundry Inc. in Rumsey, California. He is the designer of the ITC Stone, Stone Print, Silica, Cycles, Arepo, and Basalt typeface families. Mr. Stone was the art director and one of the designers of the prize winning ITC Bodoni. Recent projects include the design of initials for the Arion Press Bible and the revival of Frederic Goudy's Scripps College Old Style type. Mr. Stone is also the author of *On Stone: The Art and Use of Typography on the Personal Computer*. From 1984 to 1989 Mr. Stone was Director of Typography for Adobe Systems, Inc., Mountain View, California where he conceived and implemented Adobe's typographic program including the Adobe Originals. He has served on

the board of the Association Typographique Internationale (ATypI) and as the editor of its journal, *Type*. Mr. Stone's background includes training and experience as a mathematician, type designer, calligrapher, graphic designer, teacher, and organic farmer. His education in the graphic arts began when he studied calligraphy with Lloyd Reynolds at Reed College in Portland, Oregon. He has taught lettering, typography, and type design at various institutions, and has written and lectured extensively in the field of typography and design.

LAURIE SZUJEWSKA is the principal of shoe yéf skä design, a firm specializing in graphic design and typography. Szujewska received her MFA in Graphic Design from the Yale School of Art, where she studied with Paul Rand, Bradbury Thompson, Wolfgang Weingart, Armin Hofmann and Edward Tufte. She joined Silicon Valley's Adobe Systems early in its formation, serving as art director in the type products division under the leadership of Sumner Stone. Szujewska was responsible for the design of the award-winning Adobe Originals type specimen book series, the magazine *Font and Function*, and the creation of the typeface Giddyup. She worked with Carol Twombly, Max Caflisch, and Jack Stauffacher, who continues to serve as her mentor. The recipient of numerous design awards, she has taught design and typography at the California College of Arts and Crafts in San Francisco and at the Minneapolis College of Art and Design. She also studied and maintained a studio at the Center for Book Arts, New York City. Szujewska currently resides on Sonoma Mountain, north of San Francisco, where she maintains her design studio and printing press. As a naturalist at the Fairfield Osborne Nature Preserve, she teaches children about wildlife and ecology.

SUSIE TAYLOR is Curator of the Harrison Collection of Calligraphy and Lettering at the San Francisco Public Library. A calligrapher since the late 1960s, her teachers include Byron J. Macdonald, Arne Wolf, and Hermann Zapf. She is a founding member of the Friends of Calligraphy, and has served on the society's Board of Directors in various capacities, including as President, since 1976. Examples of her calligraphy have been published in *Artist & Alphabet: Twentieth Century Calligraphy and Letter Art in America, Calligraphy Today: Twentieth-Century Tradition and Practice, Contemporary Calligraphy: Modern Scribes and Lettering Artists II*, and *Alphabet, The Journal of the Friends of Calligraphy*.

Donors to the Exhibition

The Friends of Calligraphy and the Zapfest organizers are grateful to the following companies and organizations for their generous support of the exhibition and catalogue:

Apple
Condé Nast Publications
Adobe Systems Incorporated
Linotype Library GmbH
The Font Bureau, Inc.
FontShop International
The San Francisco Center for the Book
The Book Club of California
The San Francisco Public Library
Friends & Foundation of the San Francisco
    Public Library
The Marjorie G. and Carl W. Stern
    Book Arts and Special Collections Center
    of the San Francisco Library
American Printing History Association,
    Northern California Chapter
California Center for the Book
Gleeson Library Associates
Society for Calligraphy

The Friends of Calligraphy and the Zapfest organizers are grateful to the following individuals for their generous support of the exhibition and catalogue:

ZAPFINO LEVEL
Fred Brady
Helen Fung
Charles & Nancy Geschke
Linnea Lundquist &
    Ward Dunham
Doyald Young

DIOTIMA LEVEL
Terry McGrath
Taro Yamamoto

PALATINO LEVEL
Larry & Marsha Brady
Pat Buttice
Jon Harl
Jean Larcher
Jerry Lehman
Max Phillips
David Siegel
Susan Skarsgard &
    Wesley B. Tanner
Susie Taylor
Anne Yamasaki

ALCUIN LEVEL
Brian Allen
Diane Amarotico
David Ashley
Barbara Bostwick
Robert Boyd
Jane Brenner
David Brookes
Adrian Burd
Barbara Callow
Janice Carrier
Ewan Clayton
Christine Colasurdo
Patricia Jane Cooke
Thomas Costello
Claude Dieterich A.
Paul & Ginger Duensing
Becky Rose Eisenstein
Evelyn Fielden
Lefty Fontenrose
Willy Gardner
E. M. Ginger
Georgianna Greenwood
Eileen K. Gunn
JoAnne Hansen
Margaret Neiman Harber
Karen Haslag
Shirley J. R. Holland
Jocelyn Hunter
Douglas F. Jones
Jimmy Koide
Donna Lee
Virginia LeRoux
James R. Lewis
Ruby Liang
Lee Littlewood
Shirley D. Loomis
Terry Louie
Sherrie Lovler
Ernest March
Michaelynn Meyers
Carol Pallesen
Linda Race
Carl Rohrs
Beth Regardz
Star Type
Erma Takeda
Carla Tenret
Naomi Teplow
Jim Wasco
Wendy Watson
Jody Williams
David Winkler
Eleanor Wong
Maxim Zhukov

Acknowledgments and Credits

"Bookbinding, Calligraphy and Type Design: Remarks and Musings About My Design Process" by Gudrun Zapf von Hesse, originally appeared in *Calligraphy Review,* Fall 1991. Reprinted by permission of the author.

The text by Mark F. Guldin on page 31 is reprinted from *Twenty Years of the Frederic W. Goudy Award.* Rochester, New York. The Press of the Good Mountain, School of Printing Management and Sciences, Rochester Institute of Technology, 1988. Reprinted by permission.

The text by Hermann Zapf on pages 26 and 27 is reprinted from *About Alphabets: Some Marginal Notes on Type Design.* Cambridge, Massachusetts and London: MIT Press, 1970. Reprinted by permission.

The following materials are reproduced courtesy of the Hallmark Archives, Hallmark Cards, Inc.: *Favorite Bible Verses: Words of Wisdom, Strength and Praise,* page 24; *Thy Sweet Love Remembered,* page 29; photographs of Hermann Zapf, pages 25 and 28; the type specimens on pages 26, 27 and 154. All Hallmark materials are under copyright of Hallmark Cards, Inc.

Diotima® Optima® Palatino® and Zapfino® are registered trademarks and Ariadne™ and Smaragd™ are trademarks of Heidelberger Druckmaschinen AG, exclusively licensed through Linotype Library GmbH, a wholly-owned subsidiary of Heidelberger Druckmaschinen AG. Zapf Renaissance Antiqua™ is a trademark of Scangraphic Dr. Böger GmbH. Nofret™ is a trademark of Berthold Types Limited. Alcuin™ and Colombine™ are trademarks of URW++ Design and Development GmbH. Adobe Illustrator® Adobe Photoshop® Brioso® Ex Ponto® Galahad® Nyx® Voluta Script® and Waters Titling® are registered trademarks of Adobe Systems, Incorporated. FF Kosmik™ is a trademark of FontShop International. ITC Humana® ITC Kendo® and ITC Woodland® are registered trademarks of International Typeface Corporation. Hiroshige™ is a trademark of AlphaOmega Typography. Bitstream Cataneo™ is a trademark of Bitstream, Inc. Elli™ is a trademark of Harvard University, Jean Evans and The Font Bureau, Inc. Hoffmann™ is a trademark of The Font Bureau, Inc. and Richard Lipton. Other brands or product names are registered trademarks or trademarks of their respective holders.

The specimen poster of Zapfino shown on page 68 is used with the permission of Linotype Library GmbH. The specimen booklet pages of Galahad shown on pages 94 and 96, the proof of Voluta Script shown on page 140, and the specimen book pages of Ex Ponto shown on pages 142 and 144 are used with the permission of Adobe Systems, Incorporated. The specimen booklet of FF Kosmik shown on page 101 is used with the permission of FontShop International, home of the FontFont library. The specimen book page of Hoffmann shown on page 128 is used with the permission of The Font Bureau, Inc. The specimen page of Bitstream Cataneo shown on page 130 is used with the permission of Bitstream, Inc.

Photographs: Hermann Zapf and Gudrun Zapf von Hesse, pages 11, 45 and 73, by Jovica Veljović; Vietnam Veterans Memorial, page 51, by Ann Hawkins; Alan Blackman, page 95, by Michael Harvey; Erik van Blokland, page 99, by Amy Ramsey; Rick Cusick, page 103, by Jill Bell; Timothy Donaldson, page 107, by Helen Donaldson; Akira Kobayashi, page 123, by Yumiko Kobayashi; Jacqueline Sakwa, page 131, by Lisa Ryan; Robert Slimbach, page 135, by Robert Slimbach; Viktor Solt-Bittner, page 139, by Birgit Bittner; Jovica Veljović, page 143, by Jovica Veljović; Julian Waters, page 147, by Banita Cheung.

The cover art and frontispiece were digitally created by Rick Cusick using Adobe Illustrator 8 and Photoshop 5. The alphabets and texts are by Hermann Zapf and Gudrun Zapf von Hesse. On the cover, the texts by Hermann Zapf are from *Hunt Roman: The Birth of a Type* (1965); *About Alphabets: Some Marginal Notes on Type Design* (1970); and *Hermann Zapf and His Design Philosophy* (1987). The cover texts by Gudrun Zapf von Hesse are from the essay "Bookbinding, Calligraphy and Type Design: Remarks and Musings About My Design Process" (1991). The cover alphabets are Alcuin, Ariadne Initials, Comenius, Diotima, Melior, Missouri, Nofret, Optima, Shakespeare, Smaragd, Zapf Chancery, Zapf Renaissance Antiqua, and Zapfino. On the frontispiece (page 2) the alphabets are Alcuin, Diotima, Optima, Palatino, Smaragd, Zapf Chancery, and Zapfino. The frontispiece text, by Hermann Zapf, is from the afterword to *Manuale Typographicum* (1954).

Catalogue design by Jack Stauffacher and Laurie Szujewska. Set in Zapf Renaissance Antiqua. Color separations by Craig Hansen of Color Paramount, Petaluma, California. Printed on Zanders Medley Pure.

VOGUE ARCHITECTURAL DIGEST GLAMOUR Mademoiselle BRIDES SELF GQ VANITY FAIR Gourmet BON APPÉTIT Traveler allure HOUSE & GARDEN WIRED Lucky. CONDÉNET NEW YORKER

EVERYTHING YOU WANT TO KNOW

CONDÉ NAST
PUBLICATIONS

The Marjorie G. and Carl W. Stern Book Arts and Special Collections Center
San Francisco Public Library

A Department of Rare Books and Special Collections was created by City Librarian William Holman and formally dedicated in 1964. After a period of impressive growth, the renamed center – The Marjorie G. and Carl W. Stern Book Arts and Special Collections Center – reopened in April 1996 on the sixth floor of the new Main Library. Materials have not yet been completely cataloged in the Library's online system. Patrons are encouraged to search the Center's card catalog, and consult with staff. All materials are noncirculating, and must be used in the Center. Gifts and donations are an important element in the development of the collections. Interested donors may contact Book Arts and Special Collections staff for more information. Funding for the building of the Book Arts and Special Collections Center was made possible through the generosity of Marjorie G. Stern.

The Marjorie G. and Carl W. Stern
Book Arts and Special Collections Center
San Francisco Public Library
100 Larkin Street, Civic Center
San Francisco, California 94102
Telephone 415 557-4560

The Richard Harrison Collection of Calligraphy and Lettering. The Harrison Collection was organized in 1963 through the efforts of City Librarian William Holman and Theo Jung, calligrapher and book designer. With their encouragement, local calligrapher Richard Harrison donated his private collection to the library and continued to provide support throughout his lifetime. The collection contains nearly 1,000 examples of modern calligraphy, including manuscripts, broadsides, handwritten books, fine prints, drawings and sketches. Nearly one hundred individual scribes and lettering artists are represented. A reference collection of over 600 works supports the study and practice of calligraphy.

The Robert Grabhorn Collection on the History of Printing and the Development of the Book. In the 1930s, the San Francisco printer Robert Grabhorn started his book collection to study the solutions of the masters to problems of design, typography and bookmaking. By the time this printer's library was transferred to the San Francisco Public Library in 1965, it had grown to include almost every typeface, printer and publisher of note from the past five hundred years. The collection is particularly strong in early type specimens and the work of sixteenth century French and Italian masters. Also of note are fine press editions of twentieth century letterpress printers, including printers' ephemera. The collection supports the study of printing, papermaking and bookbinding with a large reference collection of books, pamphlets, and periodicals. An active acquisitions program has increased the collection to over 9,000 volumes. The Max J. Kuhl Collection and the Jane Hart Collection on Book Design are included here.

The Schmulowitz Collection of Wit and Humor (SCOWAH). San Francisco attorney Nat Schmulowitz founded this extraordinary collection in 1947 by presenting ninety-three humor books to the library. The collection now includes more than 20,000 volumes and fifty-five periodical titles in thirty-five languages. It covers a span of over 400 years, making it one of the largest collections of wit, humor and folklore in the world. Mr. Schmulowitz's sister, Kay Schmulowitz, supported the collection over the years and provided generous bequests for SCOWAH's continued development.

The James D. Phelan California Authors Collection
The George M. Fox Collection of Early Children's Books
The Robert Frost Collection
The Panama Canal Collection
The Sherlock Holmes Collection
The Little Magazine Collection

The Adobe® Type Library

Type is developed at Adobe Systems, Incorporated by a dedicated staff of designers, production specialists, software engineers, and marketing professionals. The typefaces in the Adobe Originals Collection and the Adobe Type Library have won numerous awards and are used by graphic arts professionals around the world. It is our mission to provide useful, practical and beautiful typefaces for our clients. We are proud that our library includes the OpenType® fonts shown at the right.

The Type Marketing and Type Development Staff at Adobe is proud to support the exhibition *Calligraphic Type Design in the Digital Age: An Exhibition in Honor of the Contributions of Hermann and Gudrun Zapf*

We celebrate the seminal and prodigious typefaces designed by Hermann Zapf and Gudrun Zapf von Hesse. We also celebrate the efforts of the talented type designers around the world who have been influenced and inspired by these two modern masters.

Adobe

Caflisch Script® Pro
Designed by Robert Slimbach

Calcite™ Pro
Designed by Akira Kobayashi

Adobe Caslon™ Pro
Designed by Carol Twombly

Chaparral® Pro
Designed by Carol Twombly

Adobe Garamond™ Pro
Designed by Robert Slimbach

Adobe Jenson™ Pro
Designed by Robert Slimbach

LITHOS™ PRO
Designed by Carol Twombly

Minion® Pro
Designed by Robert Slimbach

MOONGLOW™
Designed by Michael Harvey

Myriad® Pro
Designed by Robert Slimbach and Carol Twombly

Orgánica™ GMM Semiserif
Designed by Gabriel Martínez Meave

Silentium™ Pro
Designed by Jovica Veljović

Tekton® Pro
Designed by David Siegel

TRAJAN® PRO
Designed by Carol Twombly

Warnock™ Pro
Designed by Robert Slimbach